Culture, Country, City, Company, Person, Purpose, Passion, World

The Grand Strategies and Unifying Principles
Behind the Groups Which Rise and Thrive

Bill Bodri

Top Shape Publishing LLC
1135 Terminal Way Suite 209
Reno, NV 89502

ISBN-10: 0-9998330-1-4
ISBN-13: 978-0-9998330-1-8

DEDICATION

This is a book on big principles. It explains why large or small organizations of men grow with success or diminish and decline. It is for people who want to know the causes of prosperity for collections of men - how to create them, how to maintain them, and how to protect their collaborative unity and grand objectives from deterioration. It is about how to develop an auspicious future, and how to prevent a decline in fortune. If you can learn how to align with the principles of prosperity, and adapt your strategies as conditions change, then you will develop one of the most useful skills available to humanity.

CONTENTS

ACKNOWLEDGMENTS

The reason this book came into being was because my friend, Lee Shu Mei, asked me to give a lecture for Chinese entrepreneurs, businessmen and university professors to help them see the big picture of history and place themselves in the grand scheme of things. Because Communist China had opened its doors to Capitalism, at the same time she also wanted me to introduce the ideas of ethics, values, virtue, service and character.

I have had more entrepreneurs, businessmen and executives come up to me after they heard that talk, and ask me to present it within their companies (mostly to help with product creation since successful products and services embody service and merit to the public), than for anything else I ever lectured upon in China. One day I finally sat down and turned the lecture into a book because of this demand, which is what you now have in your hands. Hopefully you'll find it of value, and should know that the credit for it therefore goes to Lee Shu Mei and her original request.

1
INTRODUCTION

One of the most amazing videos you can watch on Youtube, which is also incredibly humbling, is the Sloan Digital Sky Survey of the cosmos. The video presents an accurate fly-through of the largest-ever three-dimensional map of galaxies in the universe with their correct images and approximate locations. When you think about it, each galaxy represents the potential for life, and in the video you therefore see the potential of endless life everywhere across the universe!

Upon watching such a grand view, one cannot help afterwards but to ask, "What is the purpose to it all? Our small lives are so inconsequential within this immensity, so what is the point to our lives other than just protoplasm reproducing itself?"

Scientists, philosophers and religious functionaries have been arguing over this issue seemingly forever. A common theme that consistently runs throughout their theories is that all things must have come from one single, primordial, foundational, fundamental origin. Whether we call It primal source, First Principle, Ultimate Origin, God, Allah, Parabrahman, Ein Sof, absolute essence, True Self or Buddha-nature, the common inference is that this source nature of everything is supreme, self-so, pure, eternal and unchanging.

Through various transformations and complex interactions, over time this fundamental source of ultimate changeless purity somehow formed galaxies, stars, planets and even life through the processes that we might call creation, evolution or transformation. All phenomena created through this process, which means the entire universe itself, share some common characteristics:

1. They are impermanent since they are always transforming
2. They are infinitely interconnected with one another through the network of interdependent causes and effects, with each phenomenon mutually contributing to define every other in a grand network of infinite interlinkages
3. Everything taken together (all things that we normally consider as separate, independent phenomena) must therefore be considered as one single whole due to infinite interdependence linking everything in cross-definition
4. You can only get to know about any of this because you are one of the phenomena within the whole that is lucky enough to have a mind (consciousness) able to form thoughts; your great treasure that separates you from other phenomena is consciousness, which is the ability to perceive, think, and know – you have self-awareness and can generate Knowledge

As individuals we are phenomena within this whole, just like everything else, and therefore interconnected with everything else while subject to the same laws of cause and effect. We might not know all the laws of cause and effect that affect/bind us, but we are subject to the processes of cause and effect nonetheless, which is sometimes called interdependent origination.

Now, within this giant universe that is experiencing uncountable transformations happening every moment everywhere, all subject to known and unknown laws of interdependence (cause and effect), we can simply let matters happen to us, or can try to master the changes of phenomena to make our lives better and go the way we want. I choose that path, and so should you, which is to try to become master of your fate. We can choose to either be a willing victim who simply accepts everything that comes our way from prior causes without trying to transform things into something better, or a master who tries to make things happen in the directions we want them to go. Personally, I want to know how and become skillful at always being able to guide circumstances to better states of being.

Whether there is an ultimate purpose to life or not, as sentient beings with consciousness we definitely have the ability to study and then derive the causative laws of change ruling nature, psychology, human history, and so on and then through devoted effort and intent can try to create worldly outcomes that we seek. By understanding cause and effect, you can work to improve yourself, your circumstances and phenomena to do better than just playing the cards life deals you as best you can. You can change things for the better.

On a larger scale than each of our individual lives, by studying history we can often find hidden patterns and principles that we might use together with this mindset to guide the transformations of cultures, countries, cities, communities and companies to better states. If we can decipher the principles of growth from initial beginnings to fullness and then decline, and determine how to maintain and sustain desired states such as prosperity or affluence, we will indeed possess some of the "keys to the Kingdom" in this vast melting pot of ceaseless, endless transformations.

As some would argue, there might not be an ultimate Creator or an ultimate purpose in "All of This," but we can create a personal purpose for our lives, or devote ourselves to multiple purposes within our lives, by working to bring about specific ends of our own liking. Through decision and willpower we can instill a purpose to our lives and thereby impart to it greater meaning. Our purposes can be whatever we decide them to be, and our missions whatever we decide to do. We have this ability of decision because of the gift of consciousness. All non-sentient things in the universe, which is the majority of it, must simply let events happen to them. But since they are insentient phenomena without consciousness, to them it doesn't matter – insentient means they cannot know anything. The beings with consciousness are their ultimate master.

I would argue that in the universe we are more than just the phenomenon of life which desires to prolong its survival and pass down genes. We are sentient, conscious beings who want to live life on our own terms, free of suffering and full of joy and fulfillment. We are not just seeking to live but *to thrive with happiness, prosperity and affluence.* Hence, we must seek for the principles that can bring this to our lives, our families, our communities, states, countries and cultures. Then we must make use of them.

If we can learn these principles, and then *align with the proper actions that master the changes of phenomena to produce our desired directions,* we can bring about better states of being for our communities and the world. Isn't this what we are ultimately after for ourselves and others? Don't we want to make the world a better place for ourselves and our children? Instead of a scorched earth, don't we want to leave a positive mark on the world and create a greater legacy for the coming generations? We therefore need to know the proven principles of producing prosperity if we want to become the masters of positive change.

If we have the knowledge, wisdom, willpower and opportunity, we will have the basics necessary for bringing about golden states of affluence and ascension. Here, then, are some of the principles of change that will enable you to guide the common transformations within progressively larger to smaller bodies of men, and then upwards again.

2
CULTURES & CIVILIZATION

I met a traveller from an antique land,
Who said—"Two vast and trunkless legs of stone
Stand in the desert. . . . Near them, on the sand,
Half sunk a shattered visage lies, whose frown,
And wrinkled lip, and sneer of cold command,
Tell that its sculptor well those passions read
Which yet survive, stamped on these lifeless things,
The hand that mocked them, and the heart that fed;
And on the pedestal, these words appear:
My name is Ozymandias, King of Kings;
Look on my Works, ye Mighty, and despair!
Nothing beside remains. Round the decay
Of that colossal Wreck, boundless and bare
The lone and level sands stretch far away."
- "Ozymandias," Percy Bysshe Shelley

Let us briefly peruse a list of some of the great civilizations that once spanned large parts of the world, some populated by millions during their heyday, but of whom we have scant evidence today that their greatness even once existed. Sometimes only crumbling stones leave a tale that these fallen civilizations at one time held sway over countless people and vast tracts of land:

Assyrian

CULTURE, COUNTRY, CITY, COMPANY, PERSON, PURPOSE, PASSION,
WORLD

Akkadian
Sumerian
Hittite
Bactrian
Scythian
Babylonian
Egyptian
Parthian
Medes
Harappan
Minoan
Mycenaean
Khmer
Olmec
Aztec
Mayan
Anasazi

In no particular order, here is yet another list of some of the Empires that once ruled large portions of the world, many of which are names you might recognize, but despite their previous greatness and grandeur have also become extinct:

Roman Empire
Byzantine Empire
Holy Roman Empire
Ottoman Empire
Persian Empire
Sumerian Empire
Inca Empire
Gupta Empire
Imperial China
Mongol Empire
Chola Empire
Macedonian Empire
Songhai Empire
Achaemenid Empire
Athenian-Greek Empire
Trading Empires of the Spanish and Portuguese
Empire of Aksum
Mughal Empire
Umayyad Caliphate

Russian Empire
Austro-Hungarian Empire
Alexander the Great Empire
Napoleonic Empire
Soviet Empire
British Empire
Third Reich

Whenever an arrow is shot in the air, its final destiny is certainly known
– it will rise and then fall. Similarly, empires that rise must eventually fall for
they all follow without exception the same law of causality. Greatness is
impermanent, status is impermanent, life is impermanent, existence is
impermanent.

There are a number of factors that have caused both the rise and fall of
empires and civilizations, and historians who study such matters correctly
conclude that none of them can be considered solely decisive. This is a
fascinating topic, so the big thinkers who cogitate on the causes of imperial
decline, for instance, say the determinants are never singular, nor black and
white.

The list of possible contributing reasons for the decline of empires?
There are economic, political, social, environmental and military causes
including foreign invasions, moral decline, overconfidence leading to
overextension, ethnic tensions, degradation of institutions, famines, plagues,
depleted agricultural lands, nomadic invasions, and financial ruin. These
many causes interact with one another in an interdependent, reflexive
fashion that eventually produces the fate of termination. No empire dies
due to a single cause.

Alexander Dermandt, a German professor of Ancient History in Berlin,
actually listed 210 reasons in *Der Fall Roms* that have at one time or another
been suggested to explain the decline of the Roman Empire!

More recently, in *The Rise and Fall of the Great Powers* historian Paul
Kennedy argued that over the last 500 years the great Western powers have
all consistently followed a regular pattern of imperial overstretch and
entangling alliances that forced them to spend more on defense than
appropriate, thus neglecting their domestic investment. As each great power
fell into relative economic decline its rivals saw opportunity and challenged
it with great wars that eventually bankrupted it. We could call this
overextension the result of arrogance and hubris, which the Greeks often
claimed was the forerunner of a fall.

Prabhat Rainjan Sarkar also set forth a theory of the evolution of
macrohistory (the Law of Social Change) where specific classes of
individuals assume the helm of a civilization, culture, or empire and then
lose their status of preeminence, with the baton then being passed to

another class of individuals in a consistent, repeatable pattern. In other words, various classes of people would rotate in controlling the fate of a nation with groups such as warriors (soldiers), laborers, intellectuals, or businessmen (acquisitors) taking turns at the helm as the most elite strata.

Crane Briton in *The Anatomy of Revolution* has written about the uniformities found in political revolutions that lead to the fall of controlling powers. Arnold Toynbee has also written entire volumes about the rise and fall of civilizations, which naturally disintegrate for a wide variety of reasons. Empires rise and fall, economies boom and bust, but what are the laws or principles behind these changes?

The most famous analysis of the life cycle of an empire is probably Edward Gibbon's *The History of the Decline and Fall of the Roman Empire*, written between 1776 and 1788. Although scholars still debate the causes, Gibbon is the one who popularized the field of empire analysis. His monumental scholarly work, covering approximately 1,200 years of history and necessitating several volumes, catalogued what he believed were the reasons for the rise and fall of the Roman Empire.

Ibn Khaldun

The rise and fall of great empires and civilization is a fascinating topic, and so countless scholars have studied the patterns of empires and dynasties - their growth, maturation, decline and fall. One of the most attractive patterns for explaining the rise and fall of states, empires and dynasties was developed by Ibn Khaldun, a fourteenth century Arab historian.

Ibn Khaldun noted a recurring historical pattern of state-building and collapse among Arab desert tribes that has since then become famous. He noted that a hardy pastoralist tribe from the desert would sweepingly come in and conquer farming settlements to establish a state there. Within three or four generations, however, the former tribesmen would lose their group solidarity due to their new life of greater ease and luxury. Factions would arise within their group and then they would become susceptible to a similar desert attack themselves, thus bringing an end to their dynastic reign. Ibn Khaldun developed his theory of the development and then decline of dynasties for desert tribes while Peter Turchin worked on validating this general pattern for agrarian societies.

Ibn Khaldun called a group's capacity for collective action its "asabiya," and developed a theory that its strength or weakness, improvement or decline, is the key to the fate of empires. Asabiya, which includes a feeling of unity and cohesive wholeness felt by all the members of a group, strongly develops in societies where the capacity for collective action is the key to survival. It cements the relationships and responsibilities within the group, which adds to the group's powers of persistence and survival.

Where group solidarity and cohesion are strong the asabiya of that society is strong because of the momentum of group-persistence. Where it is weak the people are weak. A group of people who show strong mutual support and cooperation with one another can facilitate coordinated action at the level of the whole society, which is necessary for empire building. People with high asabiya will readily cooperate with one another and even sacrifice themselves for the sake of the common good. High asabiya societies are therefore filled with large numbers of people strong in grit, determination, willpower, sacrifice, and group-persistence.

In such societies, little resources are given over to the production of luxuries since the focus is on survival, which requires hard work, discipline and self-sacrifice. Ibn Khaldun felt that tribes with high asabiya, who learned how to cooperate to compete and thrive under scarcity, had more success in conquering civilized people, who usually exhibit lower asabiya due to not having to face as many challenges, and could then establish a ruling dynasty over them.

According to his theories, in order for one group to conquer another, its asabiya of solidarity and coercive power must be higher. Furthermore, in order to be able to absorb other groups without its asabiya falling apart, the asabiya of the conquering/absorbing group must be stronger than the asabiyas of the lower-level groups. In short, a group with a high asabiya can more easily defend its territory and resources, and extend its sway over other groups and their resources. The "stronger asabiya conquers" principle is similar to the idea that the army with the highest morale wins the battle, although of course this is not always true. When asabiya is still high, an empire can easily reconstitute itself after a period of troubles (as the Romans would do after losing battles) but if the asabiya falls too low, the empire can self-destruct during a period of difficulties.

The penalty for being exposed to luxuries is degeneration in the strength of society's asabiya, which was forged through the struggle for survival. Ibn Khaldun observed that former conquering tribesmen in time forgot the difficult, hardening ways of the desert that made them strong, and their subsequent generations grew accustomed to a life of ever-increasing ease and luxury. Therefore, under the conditions of civilized life without deprivation group asabiya will decline and usually within four generations the descendants of the initial conquerors become so forgetful of their initial virtues that their hardiness will weaken. This is when the state collapses or is itself conquered. Ibn Khaldun found that the waxing and waning of asabiya therefore underlies imperial cycles.

The ability of an empire to expand its territory through conquest and to defend itself against enemies and threats is largely determined by many characteristics, but asabiya is a primary ingredient. Groups with high asabiya can impose their will on others and construct large empires whereas low asabiya peoples cannot since they are lacking in group unity. They lack the ability for members to cooperatively work together and sacrifice for one another. In longer-lived empires the centuries-long slow decay of asabiya occurs within the imperial cores and this adds to the conditions for decline.

Ibn Khaldun's explanation of high asabiya and its effects encapsulates some fundamental observations of history. However, asabiya is not everything. Ibn Khaldun himself noted that economic issues also lead to the disintegration of states, particularly demographically produced fiscal problems. There are many mechanisms involved in the general demographics-fiscal theory of imperial decline, but here is a simplistic outline.

Stability and internal peace within a region bring prosperity, which causes its population to increase since the people have more food to eat and aren't being killed off through wars and invasions. In other words, general prosperity in a region eventually leads to population growth, which then leads to food and resource scarcity. Overpopulation then leads to falling per capita income, lower wages, and higher land rents as scarcity sets in.

Basically, population growth gradually leads to a decline in per capita agricultural production due to the law of diminishing returns. What was once enough for the state as revenue derived from agricultural production then eventually becomes insufficient, leading to a loss of control over the military and police due to lack of funds. Public discontent about scarcity and taxes then turns into popular rebellion to accompany the fiscal insolvency, and finally you have imperial decline.

You can trace out the details of deterioration as follows. During prosperous times both the public and the rulers become used to increasing spending (luxury), and the bureaucracy and army demand more pay. As the population grows an increasing number of people seek elite positions offering the reward of power and pay from the state, while at the same time the youth in the population cannot find good employment opportunities anymore as the population expands and resources reach their limits. The limits of growth are eventually reached, which results in scarcity. Inflation rises outstripping the ability of the state to increase tax revenues, but the leadership helm will still demands its revenues because it is used to luxurious spending and doesn't want to stop. Even so, the upper classes begin to suffer from the declining revenues while the general population suffers in misery.

The governing class, ruling class or elites are a group that usually appropriated agricultural surpluses through taxes, and now they increase taxes or turn to outright confiscation to keep up the level of revenues they are used to having. The governing strata becomes an oppressor class out-of-touch with the common man and interested in scooping up as much wealth and power as possible. The increased oppression by the ruling class because of scarcity and higher spending habits leads to the ruin of the economy, state bankruptcy, political unrest, and the loss of military control. Popular discontent, and sometimes strife among the elites themselves, leads to popular rebellion and then collapse. But that's not the end of mankind because something new always replaces the old.

Dynasties may come and go, but peasants will continue to grow food, merchants will continue to trade, people will still marry and raise families, and everyone will pay taxes to whichever government or system ends up in power. This is the endless cycle of civilization. It is just that an old imperial dynasty disappears for some reason or another, perhaps being replaced by a new one, or a new system simply evolves to replace the old. Empires rise and fall, but the governing of the people simply goes to someone else.

Gaetano Mosca and Vilfredo Pareto

Historian Gaetano Mosca also rejected any theories of history that one single cause accounts for everything. He felt that a number of factors produce historical change through interdependence, none of which is solely decisive. He also came up with many useful insights on the behavior of the ruling class of elites inferred by Ibn Khaldun and the oppressed, or middle society commons, that progress to an unrest that eventually transforms into rebellion. Mosca observed that rebellions consistently involve leaders of the masses who use methods that involve "pointing out, with exaggerations, of course, the selfishness, the stupidity, the material enjoyments of the rich and the powerful; to denouncing their vices and wrongdoings, real and imaginary; and to promising to satisfy a common and widespread sense of rough-hewn justice which would like to see abolished every social distinction based upon advantage of birth and at the same time would like to see an absolutely equal distribution of pleasures and pains."[1]

This was seen in the rise of Communism and other political movements that promised Utopia to the masses. The masses are often promised by a evolutionary group that they will get free land or other privileges upon the overthrow of the old regime. *The True Believer* by Eric Hoffer gives insights into such movements. On the other hand, when a minority tribal group wants to take over the leadership helm but cannot win over the masses, it must do so by weakening the current people, break down their ethnic unity, instigate immigration to replace the current group identity, divide and

[1] James Burnham, *The Machiavellians: Defenders of Freedom,* (Putnam and Company, London, 2015), p. 76.

conquer competing groups and opposition, kill or neuter by famine, persecution or forced isolation, and promote dissension as well as hatred.

Mosca states that all societies, including democracies, are ruled by a minority. Every society is split into two classes - a class that rules and another that is ruled. This is true because without a political class there is no rule. Historical and political science is basically the study of the elite that rules, its composition, structure and its mode of relation to the non-elite, or commons. The elite, as a general rule, have the primary objective of maintaining their own power and privileges. They often have the habit of preventing others from entering their ranks, while talent from the commons below tries to force its way into the upper strata. This social mobility is necessary for a progressive society. Otherwise, the children of the elite are the only ones inheriting elite positions regardless of their own abilities and at the sacrifice of individuals of greater capacity among the non-elite, who would better serve the nation.

The elites who rule typically practice superior organizational skills, especially in gaining political power, and develop the means, which vary as the times vary, to impose their supremacy on the multitudes. As a group in power, they tend over time towards arrogance, vanity, and an undue belief in superiority and personal greatness. This tends to a hubris of behavior where the powerful work to enlarge their prerogatives that allow them to oppress and abuse others. The lesson of history is that this power must be balanced by national habits, customs, morals, institutions and especially juridical defense so that the elites cannot plunder the multitude. Juridical defense constitutes a set of impersonal restrictions on those who hold power, and thus protect individuals against the arbitrary and irresponsible exercise of power by the state and those who hold personal power.

In line with the checks and balances system created by the American forefathers in order to protect the nation from a concentration of political power, Mosca notes "History teaches that whenever, in the course of the ages, a social organization has exerted such an influence (to raise the level of civilization) in a beneficial way, it has done so because the individual and collective will of the men who have held power in their hands has been curbed and balanced by other men, who have occupied positions of absolute independence and have had no common interests with those whom they have had to curb and balance."[2] To put it another way, constraints should compel a ruling elite - who can at times exhibit limitless greed for control, domination and subjugation along with the most immoral application of brutality for its purposes - to promote the common good,

---

[2] James Burnham, *The Machiavellians: Defenders of Freedom,* (Putnam and Company, London, 2015), p. 82.

and restrain the powerful from plundering, oppressing and abusing the people. It is a common rule of behavior that even organizations and institutions charged with serving the public lose sight of their original purpose over time and become self-serving. Therefore you always need to institute a system of checks and balances within a nation.

Mosca also touches upon issues related to asabiya, the two political classes observed by Ibn Khaldun, and the character or merit of a people that keeps them united or not. In Mosca's view there is always an urban class struggle between a wealthy ruling elite, or aristocratic class, and the impoverished commons but the commons are the backbone of everything. The ruling elites historically get into trouble because their primary objective is to maintain their power and privilege, and they typically end up oppressing the commons to do so. Usually the rule of governing class elites coincides with the interests of the non-elite, but sometimes it diverges and when it does that divergence fractures national asabiya, which is when we see decline.

Mosca wrote, "Among the constant facts and tendencies that are to be found in all political organisms, one is so obvious that it is apparent to the most casual eye. In all societies – from societies that are very meagerly developed and have barely attained the dawning of civilization, down to the most advanced and powerful societies – two classes of people appear – a class that rules and a class that is ruled. The first class, always the less numerous, performs all political functions, monopolizes power and enjoys the advantages that power brings, whereas the second, the more numerous class, is directed and controlled by the first, in a manner that is now more or less legal, now more or less arbitrary and violent, and supplies the first, in appearance at least, with material means of subsistence and with instrumentalities that are essential to the vitality of the political organism.

"... We all know that, in our own country, whichever it may be, the management of public affairs is in the hands of a minority of influential persons, to which management, willingly or unwillingly, the majority defer.

"... In reality the dominion of an organized minority, obeying a single impulse, over the unorganized majority in inevitable. ... A hundred men acting uniformly in concert, with a common understanding, will triumph over a thousand men who are not in accord and can therefore be dealt with one by one. Meanwhile it will be easier for the former to act in concert and have a mutual understanding simply because they are a hundred and not a thousand. It follows that the larger the political community, the smaller will the proportion of the governing minority to the governed majority be, and the more difficult will it be for the majority to organize for reaction against the minority.

"... Below the highest stratum in the ruling class, there is always, even in autocratic systems, another that is much more numerous and comprises all the capacities for leadership in the country. Without such a class any sort of social organization would be impossible. The higher stratum would not in itself be sufficient for leading and directing the activities of the masses. In the last analysis, therefore, the stability of any political organism depends on the level of morality, intelligence and activity that this second stratum has attained.[3] ... Any intellectual or moral deficiencies in this second stratum, accordingly, represent a graver danger to the political structure, and one that is harder to repair, than the presence of similar deficiencies in the few dozen persons who control the workings of the state machine."[4]

Machiavelli taught rulers how to control the masses just as ancient Greek and Roman texts taught the nobles how to manage slaves and conquered populations. Edward Bernays, in his famous book *Propaganda* wrote, "The conscious and intelligent manipulation of the organized habits and opinions of the masses is an important element in democratic society. Those who manipulate this unseen mechanism of society constitute an invisible government which is the true ruling power of our country.

"We are governed, our minds are molded, our tastes formed, our ideas suggested, largely by men we have never heard of. This is a logical result of the way in which our democratic society is organized. Vast numbers of human beings must cooperate in this manner if they are to live together as a smoothly functioning society. ...

"It remains a fact that in almost every act of our daily lives, whether in the sphere of politics or business, in our social conduct or our ethical thinking, we are dominated by the relatively small number of persons, ... who understand the mental processes and social patterns of the masses. It is they who pull the wires which control the public mind, who harness old social forces and contrive new ways to bind and guide the world."[5] Thus even the modern Bernays confirmed the existence of an elite who try to institute control and guidance, even if in the shadows.

Gaetano Mosca and Vilfredo Pareto both developed political theories that historical change was due to the circulation of elites within societies who eventually plunder the wealth of the other classes and are then deposed in response. In fact, it is a frequent theme commonly portrayed in movies that societies develop elite leisure classes that eventually plunder the wealth of other classes, and become predatory. In short, the elites hold

---

[3] I would call this their virtue.

[4] James Burnham, *The Machiavellians: Defenders of Freedom*, (Putnam and Company, London, 2015), pp. 64, 65, 67.

[5] Edward Bernays, *Propaganda*, (Ig Publishing, Brooklyn: NY, 2005), pp. 37-38.

power while the commoners are workers who produce goods. When the privileged elites enrich themselves so that the rest of the population becomes impoverished then the inequality of wealth corrodes the asabiya of social cooperation. History shows that the concentration of wealth is natural and inevitable, but periodically alleviated by a compulsive violent or peaceful redistribution.

Countries typically grow rich when you can restrain the powerful from plundering people, such as by enforcing the rule of law that protects peoples' assets. One needs constraints such as traditions, laws and institutions to compel a ruling elite to promote the common good rather than its own good. If the elites extract too much from the common man, the concentration of wealth and inequality of income will cause internal asabiya fractures that will inevitably produce decline. Inequality corrodes cooperation, and cooperation is asabiya. Without the internal cohesion of cooperation, societies always deteriorate and disintegrate. Their existence as communities depends upon the asabiya of social connectedness.

What holds a society together in unity is group cooperation and when countries lose their ability to cooperate at the level of the whole society – which includes elites together with the commons – they break down. This is why these observations on the behavior of elites versus the commons are important. The lesson for countries is the need to reduce social inequality and wealth/income inequality, and by laws of checks and balances to prevent elites from ascending into arrogant hubris and oppressing society. Even Plutarch warned, "An imbalance between rich and poor is the oldest and most fatal ailment of all republics." One should also not allow societies to fracture because internal groups promote disunity, but must prevent social disruptions that pit groups and classes against each other.

Glubb Pasha

Sir John Glubb (1897-1987), better known as Glubb Pasha, was a British military officer and historian who offered another view on political change and different reasons for the dissolution of empires. Pasha described a general pattern in the history of fallen empires noting that they passed through a relatively consistent general life cycle of stages as they were born, expanded, matured, declined, and then collapsed.

One of the first things Pasha noted was that many empires had a lifespan of around 250 years, which is roughly ten generations. According to his estimates the Assyrian Empire lasted 247 years, the Persian 208 years, Greek 231 years, Roman Empire 233 years, Arab Empire 246 years, Mameluke 267 years, Ottoman approximately 250 years, Spanish about 250 years, Romanov Russian Empire around 234 years, and British Empire approximately 250 years.

Glubb wrote, "Every race on earth has distinctive characteristics. Some have been distinguished in philosophy, some in administration, some in romance, poetry or religion, some in their legal system. During the preeminence of each culture, its distinctive characteristics are carried by it far and wide across the world.

"If the same nation were to retain its domination indefinitely, its peculiar qualities would permanently characterize the whole human race. Under the system of empires each lasting for 250 years, the sovereign race has time to spread its particular virtues far and wide. Then, however, another people, with entirely different peculiarities, takes its place, and its virtues and accomplishments are likewise disseminated. By this system, each of the innumerable races of the world enjoys a period of greatness, during which its peculiar qualities are placed at the service of mankind."[6]

Glubb Pasha generalized a common pattern or life cycle to characterize the growth and then degeneration of many empires. The pattern involved empires similarly proceeding through a seven stage sequence of changes: (1) an age of outburst or pioneers, (2) an age of conquests, (3) an age of commerce, (4) an age of affluence, (5) age of intellect, (6) age of decadence, and (7) an age of decline and collapse.

In the first two ages, Pasha observed that a small and insignificant nation suddenly bursts forth with wild courage and energy and overruns large areas of the world through conquest. Examples include the rise of Macedon because of Philip II and Alexander the Great, the Arab empire established because of Mohammed, the ascension of Spain due to Cortez's conquest of Mexico, and the rise of the Mongols.

This is an age of heroes because the warrior conquerors are normally poor but extremely resourceful, full of energy and courage, daring, adventuresome and aggressive. Roman aristocrats, for instance, fiercely competed for status among themselves and their pursuit of fame through conquest helped to drive Roman expansion. With fearless initiative, in the age of heroes men tend to overthrow wealthy but defensive-minded empires, and as they gain power they set out to conquer more and more foreign lands.

Eventually businessmen take over at the highest levels of society during the two next stages of development, the empire ages of commerce and affluence. Commerce becomes dominant as vast areas of land now united as a single territory under one government become internally peaceful, and thus present the opportunity of an extremely large open market that can give rise to commercial prosperity.

---

[6] Sir John Glubb, *The Fate of Empires and Search for Survival*, (William Blackwood & Sons, Scotland, 1977), pp. 5-6.

By providing internal peace and security to vast areas of territory, an empire provides tremendous advantages to the field of commerce. For instance, merchants and traders can now deal with a single currency and administrative system that obviously cuts their costs. Their transportation routes are safer too. The public at this time turns its sights to making money because of the many new opportunities whereas glory and honor were the principal ambitions at the previous stage of development. So strong becomes this desire to make money that the wealthy of an empire, at this time, start to establish profitable enterprises in far corners of the earth in search of new forms of wealth.

Society, growing affluent from the spread of business commerce that takes advantage of the internal peace, and weary of taking unnecessary risks, now values material success while it downplays the values of the soldier. Military patriotism therefore loses some of its shine. The sense of duty and devotion to public service drops away because of increasing selfishness and the natural desire to become rich and enjoy a life of ease. Schools stop producing brave patriots while students start seeking the academic qualifications that will reward them with the highest possible salaries.

Ibn Khaldun would label this phase as the initial seeds of decline because it indicates a weakening of the cohesive sturdy asabiya of the empire. People who were once brave and hardy enough to carve out the territories of the empire now seek a life of ease and luxury.

As the commercial classes grow rich through trade and by cultivating natural resources, the empire starts to spend more money to build communications and transportation infrastructure in modes that befit the age. Great cities grow that are characterized by municipal magnificence in art, architecture and luxuries. Ample money gives birth to new triumphs in civilization, culture and the arts. However, moral decline accompanies this magnificence in human progress as the pursuit of wealth replaces the ideals of service, honor and adventure in the aspirations of men.

Men no longer try to bring grandeur to their country by seeking conquered wealth for their community or country, but seek it for themselves as a private interest. Virtue becomes secondary to the self-oriented desire to become personally rich, and with those riches the empire turns to defensiveness in order to retain its wealth and luxury. To justify its pacifistic departure from its historical aggressive traditions, militarism and aggressiveness are now denounced as immoral.

Conquest and business investment made possible by the empire's unity builds the wealth that leads to the next age of intellect. Through the amassing of great wealth, ample funds now become available for the pursuit of knowledge. During this fifth stage of development, rich patrons seeking fame and praise sponsor works of art, music and literature and endow institutions of learning. The empire spends large sums of money to establish educational institutions such as colleges, universities and high schools.

At its beginnings society saw popular enthusiasm for the pursuit of military glory, next it saw popular enthusiasm for the accumulation of wealth, and now men pursue academic fame and honor. The heroes of the empire change over time as do the values of the people. Where pioneers and explorers, soldiers, military glory, and builders were first admired, this changes to admiration for successful businessmen and entrepreneurs who amass wealth, and then finally academics and intellectuals (academic fame). During the final stages of the empire's decadence and decline, the most admired members of society become athletes, musicians, actors and celebrities. This high admiration for empty accomplishment exposes a shallowness that typically accompanies cultural decline.

During the age of intellect, surprising advances are often made in the fields of academics and natural science. However, just as in the case of ancient Athens, when the emphasis turns to intellectual debate and discussion then the tendency for action wanes greatly. Discussions and arguments abound where there is endless talking but no action takes place, and so public affairs worsen due to the predominance of incessant discussion without any movement forward.

In the age of intellectual achievements, cynical intellectuals and argumentative skeptics also now arise who oppose the values and religious beliefs of their empire's founding. Internal political divisions, rivalries and hatreds begin to intensify. Intellectual skepticism destroys the remaining asabiya of self-sacrifice, loyalty, duty and solidarity that binds the empire and brought it to greatness, setting the stage for decline. Internal political factions and dissension start to arise. Where once the empire was characterized by triumphant confidence during the ages of conquest and commerce, now you find that pessimism, materialism, sensual indulgence and frivolity all begin to pervade it.

This leads to the sixth age of decadence whereupon the empire loses its resolution and enters a stage of pronounced cultural and moral degeneration. It is as if through a "decline in merit" or "decline in virtue" that the empire suffers decline and deterioration. During this phase of decadence there appears a marked indifference to religion, increasing materialism, a decline in sexual morals (along with an increase in gay sex and an aversion to marriage in favor of "living together"), relaxation of personal discipline, and an increase in the divorce rate that undermines family stability. Men start to become economically non-productive or even destructive. Pleasure seeking, hedonistic pursuits and pessimism increase so that some people choose to drop out of society while turning to mindless entertainments. They become preoccupied with drugs, alcohol, and sexual pleasures as in Aldous Huxley's *Brave New World*, where a decadent culture becomes preoccupied with sex and mindless pop entertainment. It is as if watching the slow decline of Primetime TV content that gradually becomes riddled with overt sexual themes, cursing, rudeness, the effeminization of men, the glorification of crime and misconduct, and mindless violence.

A common characteristic of this stage is that foreigners settle in the empire's capital and major cities. The prevalence of a growing number of immigrants adulterates the homogeneity of the empire and they start to exert a political influence exceeding their proportion of the population, thus introducing cracks and divisions in the asabiya. Multiculturalism negates shared values automatically. The real issue is whether a minority or religious sect that moves into a nation will assimilate or not because too much internal diversity within a large nation often leads to destabilization, fracture and disintegration. Both the Chinese and Romans were able to solve this problem somewhat, but many nations do not.

As a related issue, members of annexed ethnicities to an empire feel little loyalty to the empire and will be reluctant to contribute resources to it. It is therefore a challenge to incorporate conquered people into a nation. Since you cannot obtain loyal recruits for the military from these groups, some empires recruited only from their core ethnicities because their primary social group was the only one they could rely upon. Only the core ethnos possesses shared historical memories along with common ancestry and linguistic, cultural and psychological characteristics that produce a measure of solidarity and unity that differentiates it from other groups.

The government at this stage, continuing to imagine that it will always be automatically rich, continues to spend lavishly on benevolent educational and medical missions, or other projects that collectively create a welfare state. A example is Rome's government-provided "bread and circuses" to keep the masses pacified through free food and entertainment. The welfare obligations at this stage swell leading to a public dependency and the recipients' common belief that the state-provided largess is their right rather than a privilege.

Notice that it took ten generations (around 250 years) for hardy pioneers to transform into people with a welfare state mentality! The generalized pattern of rise and fall, revealed in the history of countless empires, is that an empire begins through self-sacrifice and discipline, but eventually becomes undermined through the growth of wealth and comfort that gradually destroy the virtuous character values of the people who built it. Over time the country's internal unity then fractures. The final stages of existence involve a lowering of moral standards, cynicism, pessimism and frivolity.

Basically, bathing in affluence slowly dissolves the sense of duty to the common good that builds an empire. When affluence becomes the norm then people assume it to be permanent, and then sacrifice for the common good is replaced by an ethos of maximizing personal gain or self-absorbed decadence. The corrosive desire for money and material success as an end in itself, together with a rise in frivolity, selfishness, self-absorption and hedonism, eventually causes common people and upper class elites to lose their sense of duty and willingness to sacrifice for the common good that built the empire in the first place. Men who once were ready to give, sacrifice and serve through the generations become opportunity seekers ready to snatch, and along with that decline in character, virtue and self-sacrifice the merit of a people disappears.

Glubb Pasha observed that an empire affected by disintegrating morality, decadence and destruction of its asabiya grows weaker and more vulnerable to destruction by negative forces arising inside or outside of it. However, it basically erodes from within. A populace corrupted by the enjoyment of money and power for too long ends up becoming selfish and idle, unwilling to undertake sacrifices or make great efforts. If minorities coming into the fold also do not assimilate, this further weakens the unity of the collective whole. In general, for one reason or another the population gradually discards the very values of confidence, hardiness, tenacity, responsibility and self-discipline that had helped to create the empire in the first place, and then it ultimately collapses.

For each empire the causes of its final collapse are different because both internal and external causes work into the mix. You can never say that the decline is due to just one thing. Essentially, an empire that began in a violent outburst eventually passes through a state of decadence and decline and finally collapses accompanied by what we can term a lack of virtue, values or character merit. It initially emerged out of nowhere and passed through a stage of (1) pioneers, (2) commerce, (3) affluence, (4) intellectualism, (5) decadence but then, in the end, finally (6) collapses. At each stage of development the important areas of life might have seem changeless to the participants who expected to live and die under the same moral values, lifestyles, technology, and patterns of production that they saw at the beginning of their lives. However, changes do occur even if they go unnoticed by the inhabitants.

Glubb Pasha found that these six phases follow one another with remarkable regularity, in fact extraordinary exactitude. Empires experience similar stages of development and decline and many surprisingly live lives of very similar longevity.

Sima Qian

Yet another theory of historical change comes from ancient China. Sima

Qian, the Grand Historian of China, developed a theory of historical change based on the philosophy of virtue that is similar to and yet different from the idea of asabiya.

In Sima Qian's view, each new Chinese dynasty began with a sage king of great wisdom and virtue (ex. Yu of the Xia dynasty or Chen Tang of the Yin dynasty) and ended with an evil, degenerate monarch (ex. King Jie of the Xia and Chou of the Yin dynasty). Thus we could characterize the growth and decline of a dynasty as a process reflecting the slow dissolution of virtue.

Sima Qian's dynastic cycle theory of Chinese history postulates that each dynasty rises to a political, cultural and economic peak and then declines because of moral corruption, loses "the Mandate of Heaven" and falls, only to be replaced by a new dynasty to begin a new cycle. People are typically happy when the dynasty is rising and become violent or degenerate when it is in decline.

There are many theories on the reasons for the decline of countries, cultures, civilizations or dynasties. The accepted cycle is that they are born, grow and mature, reach a height and then decline to fall and die away, with historian Oswald Spengler aptly summarizing, "They (civilizations) are born, mature, and die." How and why something so grand can disappear into dust has transfixed the imaginations of many.

In Chinese thinking the strength of the asabiya would account for a portion of a dynasty's prosperity, but it would be called the "merit" of a dynasty (or kingdom) since it represents the communal ethic of mutual aid and neighborly spirit among its members. The asabiya embodies the positive character traits and virtues among the populace such as the general level of community cooperation, self-sacrifice, hardiness, self-responsibility, productivity and civic duty.

According to Chinese historical thinking, a country's people experience success when they accumulate/develop merit because of their virtues. If the merit declines – an analogy being that the asabiya weakens – then the welfare of the empire will also deteriorate. When the sovereign elites lose virtue to the extent that they start taxing people too much, let infrastructure such as roads decay, stop enforcing laws fairly, treat the people unfairly or stop protecting the people, the leadership of an old dynasty is said to lose the Mandate of Heaven because of its decline in virtuous ways. This is when it falls into the danger zone of being replaced through usurpation or rebellion. The elites make the mistake of forgetting the *Yijing's* teaching that "Those above secure their homes by kindness to those below."

This parallels the asabiya view that the rise to power is an expression of a people's character, and the softening of that character (which involves a deterioration of virtues) provides an opening for deterioration. Ibn Khaldun would say that when asabiya is strong there is legitimacy to an empire, and when it is weak dynasties fall, states crumble and a new group with a stronger asabiya rises. Chinese would describe this rise and fall in terms of merit or virtue,[7] sociologists in terms of social capital or social connectedness, and others in terms of the virtue of the people.

For instance, the Roman historian Livy also held the view that the decline of the Roman Empire was predominantly due to a decline in the morals of its citizenry. Cicero, Plutarch and Sallust also shared in such sentiments and this has been one of the most commonly cited explanations over the centuries for why Rome failed, namely that the fall was due to a fatal degeneration of morals that we might also word as a decline in virtue, ethics or merit. Confucius said that this emphasis on virtue especially applied to a kingdom's leaders and ruler, saying

> He who gains the hearts of the people will gain the kingdom, while he who loses the hearts of the people will lose the kingdom. Hence a ruler should first take pains about his own virtue. Possessing moral virtue, he will gain the people; Gaining the people he will obtain territory; Possessing territory he will obtain revenue and wealth; Having wealth, he will possess the resources for expenditure and have the means to act. Therefore virtue is the root and wealth is the consequence. If a ruler disregards the root and esteems the consequences he will only wrangle with his people and teach them to be rapacious. Thus, if a ruler thinks only of amassing wealth, the people will disperse from him, but if he disperses wealth among the people they will mass around him. And hence, a ruler's words and decrees that are contrary and unjust will be met by words that are rebellious in the same manner, and wealth that is ill-gotten or amassed by improper ways will be lost in the same manner.

The Spanish Empire

When the Spanish Empire of the 17th century was facing decline, the Spaniards compared themselves to ancient Rome and felt that part of the cure for arresting their collapse must involve shoring up the social decline in character virtues too.

As. J.H. Elliott explained, "Spaniards in the days of their greatness had seen themselves as the modern heirs of the Romans; and now, in the days

---

[7] See the story of Yuan Liao Fan, which equates a man's rise or fall to the accumulation or loss of personal virtue and merit, as discussed in *Color Me Confucius*.

of trouble, the analogy they had so confidently borrowed became distinctly uncomfortable. If they were indeed latter-day Romans, how could imperil Spain hope to escape the process of degeneration and decline to which imperial Rome had finally succumbed?

"But no true believer could fully accept the determinist implications of the concept of decline, and room therefore had always to be found for the possibility of divine intervention. This was where the story acquired a moral dimension. Seventeenth-century Spaniards who drew the parallels between Rome and Spain were well aware that the Roman Empire had been subverted from within by the decline of moral standards – by luxury, greed, effeminacy, and the abandonment of the traditional moral and martial virtues that had given Rome its greatness – and they saw a similar process at work in their own society. This meant that, alongside their elaborate schemes for economic and fiscal reform, they also campaigned for a reform of manners and morals as being at least equally important for the salvation of their country. Only the abandonment of public and private vices, and moral renewal, could 'oblige' God, in the seventeenth-century phraseology, to come to the rescue of His chosen people and save them from the otherwise irreversible degenerative process to which, like all natural and political bodies, Spain was prone.

"In the first two decades of the seventeenth century, therefore, we see the creation of an intellectual or mental climate in which the two predominant elements of *pessimism* and *reformism* were more or less equally balanced. Spain was sinking – but it might yet, if it followed the right course, save itself."[8]

The Spanish case once again shows a recognition that weakening virtues and increasing character faults within a population can contribute to national decline. This is a decline in merit as well as asabiya. Since asabiya is a measure of the internal strength and unity of a people, including its virtues of cooperation and sacrifice for one another, the natural question is how to increase asabiya? Put another way, how do you increase national hardiness, capability, collectiveness and unity?

People grow stronger and tighter when they consolidate against a foreign enemy in war. If you pose an external threat to a population it will tend to unite against it. However, religion is the most common way of creating asabiya among a people because it can make common convictions pervasive throughout society. Religion is a glue proven able to hold together a polyglot of people fostering different ideals. It offers an integrative spiritual ideology that engenders cooperation at a very large scale between different ethnic communities, and can unite them despite overt differences. It can

---

[8] *Grand Strategy in War and Peace*, ed. by Paul Kennedy, (Yale University Press, New Haven, 1991), pp. 90-91.

make a society of disparate elements come together as a whole. The essential characteristic of cooperation is that it requires some type of sacrifice, and the question then is for what?

Let's look at why people join a group in the first place. It is not just because of an attractive ideology, but because of the benefits it provides. People feel a sense of belonging within a group and pledge fidelity when they feel closeness to its members, when they feel safety within it, and when they feel they are sharing/producing a brighter future together. Once someone is attracted to a group, for whatever reason, it is those feelings of closeness, safety and of sharing a better future that build a community, and which can attract people into becoming members and contributing.

Why Christianity Isn't Extinct

For instance, people are often puzzled as to why Christianity survived and thrived when it could just as easily been marginalized or become extinct as has happened with many other religions. Why was it successful? Sociologist Rodney Stark suggests that the reason Christianity took hold was because it offered a better, more secure way of life than paganism. Its faith also offered a more promising vision of the future. Its advantages over paganism also included a sense of community closeness and emotional security because its members helped one another, were protected by one another to provide safety, and were equally promised a share in a heavenly future if they practiced virtue. Through Christianity, people united into a single moral community that provided advantages both in the here and now and thereafter. It created bonds of safety, identity and trust.

Women also received a special degree of respect and protection within Christian communities that was not found elsewhere, and Christians served as a stronghold of mutual aid when members experienced troubles. People in Christian communities bound together and offered compassionate service to those suffering in need. No doubt this attracted adherents. An example is the compassionate care shown by Christians for group members during epidemics or after fires. The pagans worshipping the Greco-Roman gods in their households received no such community benefits. Christians as a group demonstrated an asabiya of selfless care and sacrifice for one another that paganism could not compete against.

Together with higher fertility rates because more women were attracted to the religion, all these factors helped Christianity to prosper. Fertility rates, or population growth, were definitely one of the reasons behind its survival too. Just as different nations have a different asabiya accounting for why some rise and others decline, from this example we can see that religions do too.

War and religion are common glues that help hold together disparate groups of people and meld them into one. However, through careful measures that encourage community closeness, promise safety in unity and a better shared future you can also bring about a strong national asabiya. How does one create such a unity? To do so one needs a grand strategy.

Grand Strategy

When we look at conquering nations, they often proclaim they have some type of higher mission as the rationale for their subjugations. Their common excuse is that they have a mission they must execute for themselves or the world. Rome, for instance, believed it had a civilizing mission and that only under Roman rule could the world experience order, flourish and prosper. But also, many of its nobles were driven to act based upon the desire to win glory for themselves and Rome. "For the glory of Rome" sometimes meant, "I am doing this for my own glory as an individual."

The Spanish coated their conquest of the Americas with that idea that it was to convert the indigenous people to Christianity, thus making Spain "the vicar of God" in the New World. Much later, European powers used such justifications as well, such as when England justified the conquest of Ireland by also claiming its aim was to spread Christianity.

European nations conquered Africa with the justification that they had a moral requirement to civilize the African natives. For instance, European colonialism was peppered with talk about "The White Man's Burden," which was to "civilize lesser people." France, as an example, stood behind a *mission civilisatrice* ("civilizing mission") to justify its colonization efforts. Even so, all these calls to "civilize and Christianize" were really just smokescreens behind a desire for more resources, revenues and power. Even Islam used the "holy excuse" of spreading the teachings of Mohammed to mask its bloodthirsty plundering of India. As Saul Alinsky once commented, "All effective actions require the passport of morality. You do what you can and clothe it in moral garments ... moral rationalization is indispensible at times of action, whether to justify the selection or the use of ends and means." Thus, people have justified rulership, military conquests and expansionism or other "determinations to act" with all sorts of rationales along the lines of divine right, racial myths, manifest destiny, blood descent, the natural prerogative of a superior race, spreading civilization or some other moral mission.

The United States has a history and culture of democracy, individual freedom and religious pluralism, and has often used its creed of freedom and equality to intervene in other nations. While America has often said that part of its mission was to "liberate" nations, discipline "rogue regimes" or "spread democracy" across the world, there have always been other motives behind its many interventions.

It is fascinating that every culture has an ideological base from which it executes grand strategy, and uses it to justify its motives for conquest. Each nation, empire, culture and civilization marches according to its own unique ideological base from which cultural movements, assumptions and policies are made. A dominant ideology is always ingrained within the culture and politics of an empire/nation and presents itself as the supreme system for understanding and directing social life as well as for justifying actions.

When in an expansive mode, the men of an empire or nation, great and small, end up acting under the influence of one idea from within this ideology, the purity of which guides the nation in its efforts such as the idea of Manifest Destiny in America. That idea propels the empire forward, giving it a justified mission, and insures that it does not stay static in one stage of development for too long.

Joseph Campbell, in *The Masks of God*, noted the critical importance of ideology in this movement of nations: "The rise and fall of civilizations in the long run, broad course of history can be seen to have been largely a function of the integrity and cogency of their supporting cannons of myth, for not authority but aspiration is the motivator, builder and transformer of civilization. A mythological canon is an organization of symbols, ineffable in import, by which the energies of aspiration are evoked and fathered toward a focus."[9] This is why leaders often use the symbols of mythos to coalesce and lead a nation. The magical musical pieces of Richard Wagner are an example that comes to mind.

John Boyd concluded that moving people in a certain direction, such as motivating people to liberate the Holy Lands in a crusade, required a grand strategy developed and executed by the leaders of the movement. Its characteristics?

> What is needed is a vision rooted in human nature so noble, so attractive that is not only attracts the uncommitted and magnifies the spirit and strength of its adherents, but also undermines the dedication and strength and determination of any competitors or adversaries. Moreover, such a unifying notion should be so compelling that it acts as a catalyst or beacon around which to evolve those qualities that permit a collective entity or organic whole to improve its statue in the scheme of things.[10]

---

[9] Joseph Campbell, *The Masks of God*, (Viking, New York, 1968), 4:5.
[10] Chet Richards, *Certain to Win: The Strategy of John Boyd Applied to Business*, (Xlibris, 2004), p. 75.

In my view, each nation has an inherent spiritual greatness within itself that aspires to reach new heights in the economic, cultural, political, social, artistic and other spheres. However, every country/empire needs a grand strategy to guide its development to the highest heights by encouraging these impulses to express themselves in the highest directions. It needs a grand strategy to bring out the country's magnificence. It needs to prepare an atmosphere that allows the majestic within the people to shine. It needs a grand strategy for the preservation, betterment and enhancement of the nation's best interests that connects its people to a larger development story bigger than themselves. It needs a unifying development vision and destination promise that taps into the DNA of the country's culture, but seeks to elevates it and ennoble man, thus bringing the country to a new and higher stage where it can seed the world with characteristics so good they cannot be ignored. Therefore a grand strategy should encompass the following characteristics:

A vision rooted in human nature and the deep essence of the country (culture, group, empire) that is so noble and inspiring that it not only attracts the uncommitted and lethargic, but also undermines the opposition of pessimists, cynics, oppositionists and other adversarial naysayers. This grand notion of shared purpose should be so attractive and compelling that the entire country (culture, group, empire, community) becomes united and committed under its ideal.

The mission promise of magnificence should enervate both the inner and outer life, and entail an intergenerational contract of social motivity. It should act as a beacon, catalyst or guide around which to evolve in the nation those qualities that permit the collective whole to improve its stature in the grand scheme of things. It should insure that the community does not stay too long at one stage of development but decidedly progresses to advance forward.

Allowing people to connect themselves to a destiny story greater than themselves that resonates with glory, it should magnify the spirit of adherents who share in its participation, yet allow everyone to freely retain their own individual distinctive characteristics. It permits and empowers every person to enhance and perfect their own unique skills, interests and contributions within the larger narrative of the cohesive guiding vision.

A grand strategy provides a framework to develop not just the cultural but the economic resources of a country, and should also guide politics and the formulation of foreign policy. As a vision of idealistic but realistic national possibility, it entices voluntary participation because of its overwhelming magnificence, and a voluntary willingness to endure hardship and sacrifice to achieve it. Its integrating ideology should embody stable ideals that can slowly alter the whole fabric of society for the better, uplifting the nation. It should enable the public to release a wide variety of creative powers that produce a high measure of material and cultural advance, thus uplifting the level of civilization.

Characterized by voluntary participation rather than a prison of coerced participation (such as in Communism or the Nazi movement), it should especially champion personal liberty, freedom of choice and individual independence even though it embodies a guiding concept of group solidarity. By positioning its constructive goals in a voluntary participatory environment of mutual respect for participants that entails the highest virtues and values, it uplifts community ethics and enhances cooperation. By proposing an enticing vision of national significance powered by voluntary participation, it encourages the aggregate of personal strengths to produce magnificent social benefits. One can say that a proper grand strategy "leads a country to magnificence," or "releases its magnificence." It lets a million different flowers bloom.

If you are working on developing a grand strategy of development to lead your country forward, these are the issues to consider in trying to bring about a future worth creating. You need to create a motivating social force that lasts through successive generations, and therefore champions long-lived beneficial memes that will endure through accurate replication many times in succession. It must thrive on the internal life energy of the people and through idealistic aims lift them higher, nourishing both individual and group social undertakings while being flexible enough to retain cohesion and power through the many transformations it will experience over time. As Pulitzer Prize winner Chris Hedges has said, "The measure of a civilization is its compassion, not its speed or ability to consume" and our modern term for that is merit. Thus, a grand strategy should at its essence possess a strong moral core and be built around the concept of creating value or merit for a people, unleashing their incredible talents. It must have a purpose of bringing people to a greater magnificence of virtuous prosperity by stressing self-development that allows human powers to be their most productive. Over time a country will produce a society that lives in a manner consistent with its larger vision, such as the Italian ideal of "the Good Life."

Once established, a nation, empire, religion or other large community should then create simple beacons that reinforce focus, attention and engagement on the common shared goal that will bring it forward. In business this is called everyday reinforcement. Daniel Coyle noted, "Successful cultures do this by relentlessly seeking ways to tell and retell their story. To do this, they build what we'll call high-purpose environments.

"High-purpose environments are filled with small, vivid signals designed to create a link between the present moment and a future ideal. (They work by delivering an unbroken array of consistent little signals.) They provide the two simple locators that every navigation process requires: *Here is where we are* and *Here is where we want to go*. The surprising thing, from a scientific point of view, is how responsive we are to this pattern of signaling."[11] When we look at the symbols used to cement the German people together and guide them into wanting to build a Third Reich, one can see that countless reinforcing signals were created to fashion a willful force.

Even though cultures and religions strive to do this, they are still subject to the laws of impermanence which stipulate they are destined to one day die away. For instance, Zoroastrianism, the ancient Egyptian religion, and the Greek Mystery schools along with countless other religions once predominated civilizations but are now gone without a trace. Equally important as to why they died is determining the principles behind why some civilizations, cultures and religions have survived ... what principles have prolonged their survival?

Why the Chinese Culture Survived

Perhaps the common most query along these lines is why the 5000-year old Chinese civilization, which has been subject to countless wars, invasions, plagues, droughts, famines and other catastrophes over the millennium, hasn't disintegrated? The consistent answer provided by scholars is that its survival has been due to a mixture of factors, but predominantly four.

Chinese civilization has seen longevity for the following four main reasons. First, because China itself became a unified country instead of remaining at the stage of countless fractured little states as in India's history. It unified these small states and the Chinese civilization achieved a cohesive unity of the culture through that unified assemblage.

Second, China adopted a single language that survived centuries of changes because it separated the spoken word from the written word, thus allowing for different dialects to develop over time while retaining the unifying singular literature base for easy communication.

Third, China developed an assimilation culture like a melting pot where many different ethnic groups such as the Han Chinese, Mongolians, Buddhists, Moslems and other groups were all absorbed into one. This

---

[11] Daniel Coyle, *The Culture Code: The Secrets of Highly Successful Groups*, (Random House Business Books, London, 2018), p. 180.

enabled it to prevent dissolution over time due to the entry of foreigners within its borders.

Lastly, it remained in control of its own cultural story, writing its own history rather than having its story defined by foreigners as happened with India, whose histories were initially written by the British. When a nation writes its own history it can create its own mechanism for instilling unity, as can be seen in the work done by Livy for Rome. These are some of the reasons why the Chinese culture has remained strong.

These observations focus on culture being the root of longevity whereas most scholars would typically focus on economic, political, military and other causes. For instance, it is often asked how Byzantium endured for 1,000 years after the fall of Rome. The scholarly answers will usually include references to a stable currency, safe trading routes and markets, pervasive tax collection to fund defense, and multiple pathways of social mobility (via the church, military and civil bureaucracy) that allowed breathing room for aspiring individuals to rise and make their mark in life. However, even this last answer has to do with culture. Men from poor provincial towns and villages could rise to positions of wealth, power and influence via joining the church, military and civil bureaucracies, and there were enough opportunities in social mobility that there was no reason for the culture to fracture from thwarted ambitions, which would have lead to entrenched inequalities. When there is little chance for social mobility there is little reason to contribute to a system that benefits the few (the entrenched elites) at the expense of the many. Insuring social mobility should be a top tier priority if a nation wants to become wealthy, for allowing individuals to become rich and join the class of upper elites powers the ambitions of affluence that will, in turn, bring wealth into the nation.

The central idea in many of these theories of development is that the unity of shared purpose and group-persistence along those lines produces greatness. Unity of people is known as asabiya, and alternatively as its merit, virtue, social capital, or "having a strong culture." It is a measure of the strength of group-persistence. The Chinese call the strength of the asabiya the merit of a dynasty or civilization, with the idea being that after the merit is used up an empire or dynasty declines.

Another common idea explaining the rise and fall of countries, empires and civilizations is that a growing separation between the elites and common man (often revealed by wage inequalities or large wealth disparities) destroys the unity of asabiya. When group cohesion fractures you afterwards see decline.

There are many theories about the causes behind the rise and fall of dynasties, empires, cultures and civilizations, but what one should worry about is what you can do something about ... but do not. What must be done at this moment that your nation is not doing?

Decline is usually accompanied by a general complacency in the public about the status a nation has achieved, along with a sclerosis preventing the undertaking of reforms to fix what has gone wrong. Individuals enjoying the good life have a tendency to expect the status quo to continue so they often refuse to look the trends of crumbling decline squarely in the face and rally themselves along with others to combat them.

In particular, they must especially work to prevent various parties from fomenting division within society and creating disunity within a nation, which would fracture its asabiya and enable minority groups, who organize with efficiency like tribes, to advance their interests and gain power. Men who only pursue their own self-interests rather than efforts that help the group as a whole are a common characteristic of cultures in decline.

3

COUNTRIES

"Empires wax and wane, states cleave asunder and coalesce."
- *Romance of the Three Kingdoms*

"God has granted the boon of perpetuity to no civilization, culture, country, empire, race or religion. Regardless of their military might, economic might, territorial size or total population, no such entity lasts in perpetuity."

Empires rise and empires fall, countries ascend and countries decline. The dance of history is that impermanence characterizes everything, even the ranking or pecking order of the world's superpowers swings to the left or right.

While the United States is presently the world's reigning superpower – which means a state that greatly exceeds all others along military, economic and political axes of power - previous to its ascendancy we saw Great Britain as the world's most dominant power. Before Britain the predominant leaders of the West were Spain and the Netherlands (Dutch Republic), while the leading power prior to their ascendancy was Portugal. Even earlier the dominant role belonged to Venice, whose preeminence was due to its leading role in the world's spice trade. In the East the rankings over time would be different, but no doubt featured China as predominant for some time.

There are many requirements that a nation must satisfy in order to become the leading power of the age other than just having tremendous military strength. History shows the following common requirements or patterns necessary before a country can become a dominant world leader:

- Agricultural self-sufficiency (secure food production or food sourcing sufficient for the population).
- Internal conflicts are resolved that might impede social unity (asabiya), produce coups or thwart industrialization efforts, which are often opposed by agriculturalists. Civil wars must be avoided and the country must avoid bad governance.
- Wealth accumulates based upon the country's ability to produce real valuable goods (that can compete with those of other nations). Value lies in the production of real goods and services. Debt is not wealth.
- The country demonstrates a clear evolution toward capitalist tendencies and free trade. The initial thrust to world dominance requires an increasingly capitalistic approach because it necessitates the unleashing of entrepreneurial forces based on individual decisions and proclivities. Countries grow rich through capitalism so the wisest ones don't impede entrepreneurship but encourage it. Rich countries create environments that encourage commerce and investment.
- The nation is isolated from the center of world events (such as the past cases of Britain and Spain, which is geographically isolated from the rest of Europe by being on the Iberian Peninsula) or protected geographically, politically, and economically so that it can develop without disruptions and interferences caused by other nations.
- The country is independent of direct foreign influences (the country is not under any other nation's control).
- Its land acquisition and widening sphere of influence, which help produce self-sufficiency, are not blocked by the current world leader or other nations during its pre-supremacy era.

The Chinese sage Kuan Tzu, China's foremost geopolitical strategist and the first Keynesian-monetarist in world history, explained that each country of the world (or state within a kingdom) needs a survival strategy. It needs a strategy for competing with greater and lesser states, for projecting influence in the world, and for becoming a hegemon. From choice passages of the *Kuan Tzu* we can understand some of the strategies that he advised:

A strong state gains by winning the loyalty of small states, but fails if it becomes too arrogant. A small state gains by temporarily yielding to the big powers, but fails if it breaks with its strong neighbors. Countries, whether large or small and strong or weak, each have their own particular circumstances and individual strategies for ensuring their preservation. Subjugating the neighboring states are the methods employed by the country of a king. To unite the smaller states in order to attack the larger is the method used by rival states. To maneuver the small states on one's borders to attack the other small states on one's borders is the means used by a central state. To conserve its resources and humbly serve the strong so as to avoid offending them is the means used by a weak state. Since time immemorial, no state that took initiatives against its circumstances at an improper time has ever been able to keep its name and standing. There has never been a state that did not suffer defeat after having encountered difficulties and gone against the times in attempting too large an alternation of its conditions.

He who would excel at rulership relies on the preponderance of large states to suppress others, and the power of strong states to weaken others. When strong states are numerous, its plan should be to unite with the strong to attack the weak in order to become a lord protector. When strong states are few, he should unite with the small to attack the large in order to become king. When strong states are many, it is foolish to talk about becoming their king. When strong states are few, it is a defeatist strategy to proclaim the way of a lord protector.

If all other states in the realm are well managed while your own state is in turmoil and upheaval, you will soon lose your state. If the lords of the other states are all on good terms with one another while your own state stands apart in isolation, you will soon lose your state. When neighboring states are all well prepared for war but yours remains at ease, your state will soon cease to exist. These three things are the signs of a state that will perish.

When a state is large but its government is unimpressive, it will eventually become smaller and smaller. However, if a state is small but its government is impressive, it will gradually grow larger and larger. If a state grows large but shows little achievement, it will become smaller again. If a state grows strong but is not well governed, it will become weaker again. If a state develops a large population which cannot be employed, its population will eventually decline. If a state becomes prestigious but neglects propriety, it will lose the respect it has earned. If a state becomes important but acts intemperately, it will lose the influence it has gained. If a state becomes rich but turns arrogant and dissolute, it will again become impoverished.

If a state's territory is extensive but not well managed, this is known as an excess of land. If its population is large but is not well employed, this is known as an excel of people. If its military forces are powerful but out of line with what is necessary, this known as an excess of the military.[12]

Kuan Tzu taught aspiring individuals how they might become the most powerful people in the land underneath a king (a lord protector), or its king. He revealed a number of strategies, contingent upon the circumstances of each type of state, by which each country could protect itself and thrive. Today we would call these "grand strategies." An aspiring statesmen should read Kuan Tzu, *T'ai Kung's Six Secret Teachings* (by Jiang Shang) and *The Three Strategies of Huang Shigong* from ancient China, all of which teach lessons on how to manage a country to a higher stage of prosperity.

All countries need a grand strategy for progress in order to excel and thrive. Traditionally grand strategies have focused primarily on the military or political sphere, but you also need grand strategies for the fields of economics, food and energy, education, health care, and especially for political moves that can make you into a superpower. A grand strategy is a blueprint or roadmap for national success, and constitutes the plan for a "Great Betterment."

How the Western Rich Countries Got Rich

In terms of the economic sphere of national wealth accumulation, the absolute best book on grand strategy economic policies that I've ever seen is *How Rich Countries Got Rich … and Why Poor Countries Stay Poor* (Erik Reinert).

Reinert's careful study of economic history accords with my own viewpoint that economic wealth can be a result of being willed and planned for, i.e. a result of conscious policy. China's great development these last few decades illustrates the truth of this view, for China focused on trade and manufacturing to build its country as Japan once did during the 1980s. If you align yourself with the correct principles of economic growth (such as avoiding extractive institutions, excessive politics obstructions and make it easier for entrepreneurs to succeed) then you can create wealth and prosperity in a country.

What are the sure principles of development?[13] Countries establish

---

[12] *Kuan Tzu*, trans. by William Bodri within *The Means to Win*, (Jain Publishing, California, 2000), pp. 114, 98, 78, 79, 85-86.
[13] See *Bankism* by Bill Bodri.

themselves firstly on an economic base; the foundation of prosperity for a country is economics. Each country has other nation states that are its competitors, some of whom are abusers who wish to dominate it or use it rather than see it rise higher and become rich, and so are anxious to conquer it or suppress it by offering misleading advice to thwart its development and keep it at a lower strata. This much is for certain: countries seeking greater prosperity need to diversify away from simple raw material, timber, mining, fishing and agricultural production (sectors with diminishing returns to scale) and move to sectors with increasing returns to scale such as manufacturing, technology, and services.

The rich countries of the West actually attained their wealth by diversifying trade within their cities, and by having their governments grant monopolies and employ tariffs to prevent cheaper imports from hurting the domestic manufacturing startups learning the ropes. The first rich countries (such as England, Holland and Italy) developed their economies through diversification and by protecting industrialization. These countries realized that selling finished products was more profitable than selling raw materials, and they employed tariffs and sanctioned monopolies to protect their early industries.

This emphasis on producing value-added goods and protecting those industries as they grow is the path to national riches, and has been followed many times in the West. Those nations which have used this plan have become wealthy including countries such as South Korea, Japan and Taiwan. America was also once highly protective of its manufacturing for over two centuries (despite Britain urging it not to do so in order to prevent the arising of a champion competitor) and only gradually opened its industries to international trade when they were ready to bear the heat of competition.

Part of becoming rich is to offer value to others through trade. You cannot become rich if you do not offer something to the rest of the world (so that their money comes into you for your products), but what you offer should be manufacturing products or other goods/services that embody increasing returns to scale production efficiencies. Only increasing returns to scale types of activity allow you to enjoy higher profit margins and make more money as you produce more. If you enjoy increasing profit margins along with increasing demand for your products/services at the same time, the multiplication of the two together produces wealth. That's the secret behind wealth accumulation.

You have to contrast this historically successful pattern of industrialization which dependably produced wealthy nations with the advice given today by the IMF to developing countries, who in the past have been encouraged to gear their entire economies to raw materials rather than diversify into manufacturing. They were/are also told not to use tariffs, subsidies or any other forms of domestic guardianship that would help protect any green shoots of local manufacturing industries. The focus on becoming wealthy should involve a thrust to develop domestic manufacturing industries, which is the means that the rich countries of the West themselves all used to grow rich. It is not that they grew rich through manufacturing. It is that they grew rich by turning to "increasing returns to scale" production activities together with an increasing demand for those products. As demand for your products grows while your margins get better, this is the formula for wealth.

Rich countries, you must note, tend to specialize in man-made (manufacturing) comparative advantages while poor countries usually focus on nature-made (raw material) products as in farming, fisheries, timber or mining. Man-made advantages lead to increasing returns to scale while commodity production (nature-made) leads to decreasing returns to scale, and impoverishes a nation over the long-run as natural resources are gradually used up or become harder and more expensive to procure. Furthermore, one can also *brand* a manufactured product by making it unique and different than every other competitor to thereby help increase its demand, but it is nearly impossible to compete on anything but price when your output is a standard commodity produced by many other world producers.

Countries seeking the road of wealth should also think of developing economic complexity (highly sophisticated and well-connected products in the economy) through diversification rather than solely relying on commodity exports, such as oil or coffee or copper. All raw material production is eventually subject to diminishing returns over time, and thus higher costs. For instance, it costs more money per bushel to grow a larger quantity of corn after the most fertile land is used up, and it is more expensive to mine additional copper as the richest ore deposits become depleted. Countries that want to experience wealth and prosperity must therefore focus on manufacturing and knowledge industries, which cause them to go up the value chain with increasing margins, and which often produce monopolistic positions. Such companies can pay higher salaries for talent, and countries grow rich when the salaries can go up rather than decline.

Another requirement for countries who want to progress is an educational policy that brings up the basic level of education in the nation, especially for girls since this will help prevent early marriages, early pregnancy, over-population and illiteracy. However, raising the educational level in a population will not help to increase its degree of wealth unless there is also an industrial policy that produces opportunities for the educated. Without internal opportunities, higher education is only likely to increase the propensity for the skilled and educated to emigrate.

Another factor is for a country to avoid debt and along these lines there are two special warnings I want to note. The first is that a country should own its central bank so that it can create interest-free money for various economic projects.[14] Japan, China, Germany and Australia are among the nations that once used this method to build their economies. The second is that it should avoid foreign loans, which means minimizing any foreign debt taken on for domestic development projects.

As Michael Perkins, author of *Confessions of an Economic Hit Man* explained, western institutions typically sell a development project or plan (that is too large) to a nation along with a loan to pay for it. When the debt cannot be serviced because the project was too big or expensive and doesn't make the returns promised, the country is forced to cut back on national services in education, health care, and government employment to pay the debt. A nation is then often forced to privatize public assets, such as mineral rights, land and water systems, that are then sold to foreign owners in order to help pay off the loan. Without the excessive debt trap, foreigners would never be able to get hold of these national riches. The excessive debt was actually part of a secretive confiscation plan. Creditors then end up exerting control over the country, and this accomplishment proceeds according to a plan that often includes bribing the local officials for their compliance. A country with too much foreign debt effectively passes into foreign ownership or control, its assets are confiscated, or it is simply crippled by the excessive debt burden unless it renegotiates its loans or declares insolvency.

There are countless books on how and why countries become rich offering recipes other than Reinert's recommendations. The field of economic histories offering advice to nations on how to become rich is almost like an industry, including titles such as *The Wealth and Poverty of Nations* (David Landes), *The Competitive Advantage of Nations* (Michael Porter), *Why Nations Fail* (Acemoglu and Robinson), *The Bottom Billion* (Paul Collier), *Guns, Germs, and Steel* (Jared Diamond), *Great Divergence* (Kenneth Pomeranz), *The Rise of the West* (William McNeill), *How the West Grew Rich* (Rosenberg and Birdzell), *How Nations Grow Rich* (Melvyn Krauss), *The Rise and Fall of Nations* (Ruchir Sharma), *Making Poor Nations Rich* (Benjamin Powell), *The Price of Prosperity* (Todd Buchholz), and *The Wealth of Nations* (Adam Smith).

Of all these authors there is one particular quote that strikes me hard, which is from David Landes, "If we learn anything from the history of economic development, it is that culture makes all the difference." Riches

---

[14] See *The Public Bank Solution* by Ellen Brown.

are not obtainable or sustainable without the appropriate cultural traits, an example being the Chinese work ethic that has lead to Chinese controlling the GDP in most of Asia, and the Protestant work ethic that valued hard work, enterprise and free market thinking much more so than the Catholic culture it displaced.

Traditional economists typically offer all sorts of well-known recipes that a nation should use to get rich such as encouraging exports, adopting technological advancements, improving productivity, educating workers, accumulating capital, defending property rights, following the rule of law, and establishing solid political, legal and economic institutions that allow entrepreneurs to flourish. All in all I still favor Reinert's *How Rich Countries Got Rich … and Why Poor Countries Stay Poor* because it analyzes how the western nations actually *did* become rich, which involves grand strategies different from what establishment players now recommend to emerging market nations.

Reinert notes that when competing nations saw a competitor doing everything right, they often tried to get them to adopt precisely the wrong policies that would economically keep them in an inferior position. Reinert's basic observation is that moving up the value chain to industrial products, because they offer increasing profit returns as the production scale increases, is the one dependable way to economic growth and prosperity. Landes also concurs that industrialization (an increasing returns to scale activity) is what made most western nations rich – "Some countries made an industrial revolution and became rich; and others did not and stayed poor."

Once again, it is instructive to notice the warning that the practices which rich western nations used to become wealthy are consistently the opposite from what establishment economists typically recommend to developing nations. It is a point to deeply ponder.

Monetary Stages of Prosperity and Decline

Wealth means money, and another important issue involving economic prosperity is maintaining the integrity of a nation's monetary system. Throughout history, many countries that grew rich ended up destroying that prosperity by bastardizing their currency. Michael Maloney studied this tendency and in the *Hidden Secrets of Money* revealed a consistent seven stage pattern to the rise and fall of national finances. He found that prosperous countries typically pass through a regular pattern of monetary history. In fact, the rise and fall of empires, nations and city-states is reflected in the fate of their monetary system regardless of the political system.

Since this pattern repeats over and over again throughout history (ancient Athens was one of the first to show this pattern) it can serve as a useful weathervane for predicting when a country will experience the decline of its currency and then economic ruin. In a sense it is reminiscent of the Greek historian Polybius's cyclical theory of political evolution which explains how democracies arise and eventually degenerate by passing through a regular, predictable series of steps. Polybius felt that democracies consistently experience well-known development phases starting from anarchy (primitive monarchy). In their development they pass through the stages of kingship (the emergence of a wise king leader), tyranny (power is assed through hereditary to the king's children), aristocracy (tyrants are overthrown), oligarchy, democracy (rule by the many) and then mob rule (the people of the state become corrupted, develop a sense of entitlement and accept the pandering of demagogues) leading to destruction.

In stage one of its growth to prosperity, Maloney noted that a country starts out by using "sound money" in its economy. This is typically either gold or silver coinage, or currency backed by hard assets such as gold and silver. The country basically bases its currency on *real assets* that are internationally traded – the precious metals - and therefore puts the national currency on sound footing.

In its second stage of economic development, the country starts to grow strongly, developing economically and socially. Because of its budding prosperity it introduces currency (monetary items backed by sound money) to facilitate trade and commerce. It also begins to take on more economic burdens by adding layers of public works to its budget.

The third stage of development involves a massive military buildup. As its economic affluence grows, so does the country's political influence and it then increases its expenditures to fund a massive military to protect itself. To fund the new expenditures, the government tinkers with ways to print more currency than can be fairly backed by its stock of real assets such as gold and silver. In other words, the currency is debased to allow more government spending without raising taxes. Another way of saying it is that war is inflationary, and historically countries have reduced the amount of precious metals in their coinage in order to pay for military expenditures.

A false prosperity next ensues due to the increase in money creation, and a typical fourth stage of development also involves war. The country puts the large army it has built up to use in a dangerous, destructive and combative foreign policy, and military expenditures explode. This creates massive funding debts and a larger budget deficit.

In the fifth stage of economic development, reality begins to catch up with the deficit spending, and the purchasing power of the nation's currency weakens dramatically. We typically see large currency debasement and inflation, especially if there have been war expenditures. In order to fund the war the country usually steals the wealth of the people through oppressive taxes and by further debasing its gold and silver coinage with base metals, or by replacing the metal currency with fiat paper currency that can be created in unlimited quantities. Naturally this gives rise to high inflation.

In the sixth stage there is a loss of faith in the devalued currency that had replaced sound money. The expanded currency supply causes a loss in its purchasing power, which is noticed by the populace and the financial markets, and this triggers a loss of faith in the currency. The monetary system then collapses under too many claims on a limited pool of sound money.

In the seventh and last stage, there is a mass movement out of the nation's fiat currency into the precious metals and other real, tangible assets that might preserve wealth. The currency collapses and gold and silver rise in price because of a consequential loss of faith in the government. Eventually a new monetary system, backed by sound money, begins anew.

Maloney notes that this process, seen time and again throughout history, transfers massive wealth into the hands of those who had the foresight to purchase gold and silver beforehand since these are the only monetary items that retains their (international) value. The basic story is that countries almost always eventually overextend themselves through excessive military expenditures, social projects, debt and currency debasement, which in turn degrades the cultural advantage/merit that the society had previously built up. Then it declines.

In ancient Rome, for instance, the Roman currency was never debased until the Second Punic War when the Carthaginian general Hannibal threatened Rome with his army. To finance a massive military effort against Hannibal, Rome began to debase the precious metals content of its coinage, thus inflating the money supply. Rome also started adopting a more militarist, expansionist worldview which eventually led it into becoming a dictatorship. Eventually the currency became so debased over time that it lost most of its value, and a tremendous inflation ensued. Martin Armstrong has traced the devaluation of Roman coinage over time in conjunction with government moves that follow the Maloney pattern. He has confirmed that human behavior tends to repeat itself over and over again.

Alexander del Mar, in his *History of Monetary Systems*, wrote "The numerary system lasted for nearly two centuries, during which all that was admirable of Roman civilization saw its origin, its growth and its maturity. When the system fell Rome had lost its liberties. The state was to grow yet more powerful and dreaded, but that state and its people were no longer one."

Paper Currency Impermanence

History shows that the average life expectancy for a paper currency is less than forty years, and fiat paper currencies throughout history have had nearly a 100% failure rate. Since most have lasted no longer than an average human lifespan, you should expect to see a major currency failure during your life. Given enough time, eventually all fiat currencies fail and therefore it is only a question of time and circumstances. Political systems always eventually abuse a currency, and a country always eventually pays the price.

Researcher Vince Cate investigated the fate of 599 paper currencies and found that every single one of the 599 paper money systems he analyzed eventually disappeared. The boon of perpetuity was granted to no one. Cate found that 28% were destroyed by war, 27% were destroyed by hyperinflation, 15% ended through acts of national independence (the new states renamed or reissued new currency), and 30% ended through monetary unions or reforms (such as the creation of the Euro).

Even if you assume that the value of a nation's paper currency will last forever, monetary scholar Edwin Vieira has pointed out that every 30-40 years the reigning world monetary system usually fails in some way, and then has to be retooled in order to start again. What, even world monetary systems fail? Yes! However, there is always an eventual end to the crisis because people need some form of money as a unit of exchange rather than rely on barter, which is the normal solution during a crisis. There is always an end to any turmoil, and then inevitably a new normal becomes established because societies cannot operate without a stable form of exchange, and so out of necessity a new one must be born. Currencies die, currencies are born and the people continue running their lives.

The same error of taking on too much debt (whether due to private sector spending, overextended entitlement programs, or military attempts at imperial hegemony) and too much money printing has been a common cause in the downfall of many monetary systems and nations. The great game of printing money cannot be played without limits forever. When governments reach the point where they are printing endlessly and heavily influencing asset prices so that no one can accurately determine true values anymore, then bubbles will form and eventually collapse in a Minsky Moment, thus destroying asset prices and economies. When governments print so much money that people lose faith in the national currency, hyperinflation can also appear and destroy a national economy.

Governments, like people, accumulate bad decisions over time which they fail to correct. They can certainly pursue policies that eventually lead to economic ruin and have done so many times throughout history. Like individuals, as time progresses they usually end up spending too much and taking on too much debt that they cannot repay. They borrow to overspend on military forays, grand domestic programs, and to buy voters or pacify populations with social programs. Historically speaking, in general empires have very commonly overextended themselves through excessive spending, unnecessary wars and various other efforts we can define as "imperil overreach." Because of their own overstretch, they typically weaken and someone overtakes them.

The extravagant spending to support all these activities can last only so long before there is finally a day of reckoning. If a government spends more than it collects in taxes then it must borrow ever-increasing amounts to pursue its projects so that citizens can live a lifestyle beyond their means. When the eventual day of reckoning comes because the debt servicing cannot be paid, an "end game" occurs where the economy tanks. Nations can even be destroyed. Many people put their heads in the sand saying this cannot possibly happen *here* - that systemic collapses cannot possibly occur to *their* country - but it happens. While John Templeton remarked, "The four most dangerous words in investing are, 'This time it's different,'" I would like to add four other dangerous words: "It can't happen here."

Carmen Reinhart and Kenneth Rogoff in their excellent book, *This Time It's Different,* wrote a policy guide for future generations related to these matters. They examined the fate of countless nations which experienced various types of financial crises and charted out the typical patterns of distress. They examined internal defaults, external defaults, banking crises, exchange rate crises and inflation crises. Many types of crisis can derail a hegemon, leading nation, or superpower, but banking crises are among the most common.

Reinhart and Rogoff found that banking crises typically lead to sovereign debt defaults (there have been 250 cases globally since 1800), and sovereign defaults typically lead to inflation (greater than 20% per year) and currency collapses. The typical tipping point when countries start seeing sovereign debt instability is when the debt/GDP ratio for a country hits 60% or higher. That's when they typically start to collapse. Once again the problem is taking on too much debt. Debt must be repaid, and if there isn't enough tax revenue or economic growth enough to pay the interest on the debt then the value of the debt will collapse. The term for this is bankruptcy.

After such catastrophes there is never an "end of the world" Armageddon but simply a period of structural readjustment when the pieces are put back together again to start anew, and the nation may be crippled for a long or short period of time according to circumstances. If the state survives then the whole multi-decade monetary cycle begins anew with the lessons being slowly forgotten as time marches on.

While we are speaking of ancient kingdoms and empires, and nations that were once world supremacy hegemons before they passed the baton, a sure conclusion to note is that you have a high probability of entering into at least one politically, economically, financially or militarily catastrophic period during your lifetime—at least one. Countries, like humans, experience growth cycles where they eventually reach a state of maturity, and then start upon a road of decline involving all sorts of causes and calamities. The fate of a monetary/banking system is one of the tip-offs for when to protect yourself by investing in the currencies of other nations and gold or silver to weather a coming storm.

Countries need to satisfy several requirements in order to become wealthy or go even further and become a superpower. They must go up the value chain in their economic output. They must also engage in the self-discipline of refraining from taking on too much debt, debasing their currency or entering into wars since this can destroy them. Inevitably, most countries fall into these traps and then follow a well-recognized pattern of decline.

Since self-restraint and avoiding the hubris that normally accompanies wealth seems to be the saving discipline that prevents disaster, as Landes noted the progress of a nation is a function of its culture or merit.

4

CYCLES

"For well over a century business cycles have run an unceasing round. They have persisted through vast economic and social changes; they have withstood countless experiments in industry, agriculture, banking, industrial relations, and public policy; they have confounded forecasters without number, belied repeated prophecies of a 'new era of prosperity' and outlived repeated forebodings of 'chronic depression.'"
- Arthur F. Burns

"Analyzing business cycles means neither more nor less than analyzing the economic process of the capitalist era. ... Cycles are not like tonsils, separable things that might be treated by themselves, but are, like the beat of the heart, of the essence of the organism that displays them."
- Joseph Schumpeter

"You may be better off or worse off at various times as you progress, but you should always align with the trend to ride upon the great forces that can produce prosperity."

The progress and prosperity of a country are not just dependent upon its policies of grand strategy or the strength of its asabiya for building the nation and getting through difficulties. Furthermore, the countries which experience the greatest prosperity do more than just adopt good policies such as promoting exports and engaging in debt restraint.

While in ancient times they turned to military conquest to rob resources from other nations, in modern times they have learned to align themselves with the largest forces of prosperity, which are trends of groundbreaking innovation that produce incredible, system-wide economic development. This has produced tremendous prosperity and advances in social welfare.

Those empires, countries and cities that aligned themselves with these forces – which determine the primary direction of economic growth over decades – have been the biggest winners in world history. Those who did not align with these forces, but shunned them, remained in poverty.

Long-term innovation waves serve as a, if not *the*, key growth process in global economics. The rise of great powers, at least in the West over the past several hundred years, can be traced back to a leading adoption of, adherence to, mastery of or promotion of these economic innovation waves. The great powers and even superpowers were the ones that astutely tapped into their buoying power and thus lifted their own fortunes to the status of preeminence.

The most important economic cycle within these long-term growth forces is the Kondratieff wave, which is on average a 40-70 year economic prosperity cycle discovered by Russian economist Nikolai Kondratieff. Sixty years is just about its average length of 57 years. Since sixty years is a good round number that also coincides with the approximate length of three generations as well as the *basic* unit of time used in the Chinese calendar system, and since it is also the length of the Saturn-Jupiter orbital cycle used in Indian calendars, most people just refer to the Kondratieff wave as a rounded sixty year cycle.

Famed economist Joseph Schumpeter taught that capitalism entails a continuous evolutionary process of innovation and "creative destruction," and the Kondratieff wave plays a key role in this birth and death process that is incessantly revolutionizing economic structures. If you can master the Kondratieff wave, which spans decades, you can master the most powerful prosperity forces within a nation. What you must do for the greatest benefit is be an adopter who taps into it early. You can come late to the game also, but the early bird gets the biggest benefit. The Kondratieff innovation waves are definitely responsible for the rise and fall of economic fortunes in various nations over time.

The Kondratieff wave, also known as a K-wave, is a very long economic wave produced by groundbreaking innovations and inventions, such as the automobile or printing press, that launch technological revolutions. Those innovations are a primary triggering force behind the establishment of new leading industries and industrial sectors that produce most of the economic growth within a country for a sustained period of time. By riding on top of a Kondratieff wave and engaging with it fully a nation can become one of the most productive economies in the world and gain competitive advantage over contenders. When a country ignores these innovations it falls behind.

To see how this works we can examine a Kondratieff wave whose strongest section occurred between the 1920s and 1950s. This period became known as the automobile era of Individual Mobility and the basic innovation that triggered this Kondratieff economic growth cycle was of course the automobile. The invention of the automobile produced two large economic sectors in the most adoptive nations - the automotive industry and the petrochemical industry since cars run on gas and oil.

For approximately half a century these two industries, and others along their value chain, attracted the most investors, produced the greatest returns and employed the most people in the nations that embraced them. They played a leading function in the adoptive economies by determining the primary direction of economic growth for decades. Commercialization of the automobile did not just result in auto sales and petrochemical development but in massive nationwide construction projects for highways, bridges and roads. This building mecca produced permanent infrastructure that became a boon to any participating economies.

Steel and tire manufacturers, oil and gas heating system manufacturers, fuel power station manufacturers, gas stations, banks, insurance companies, tourism companies and numerous other companies such as suppliers of metal, plastic and electronic parts all benefited from the bandwagon effect which uplifted any participating nations in the automobile-petroleum K-wave. An enormous network of suppliers, customers and users evolved across the globe in its wake creating prosperity as they became involved with this Kondratieff growth wave.

Thanks to the automobile and petrochemical industry many new professions were also created. Trucks made deliveries faster, greatly expanding the market area that businesses could serve. A new era of mass transit was born as cars gave people high personal mobility, which also changed society on a grand scale. Universities and all sorts of cultural efforts benefited from this new freedom of mobility. In short, the automobile-petroleum K-wave changed virtually all levels of society in the direction of greater prosperity.

The wave just prior to the automobile and petrochemical ascendancy, which started around 1870-90, was powered by scientific discoveries in electrotechnology and chemical processes. This was a time when electrical communications started spanning the globe, electric motors started replacing human muscle power, electrical lights became popular, and material living conditions improved dramatically for people due to electrical innovations. It became an era of Mass Consumption where many people received higher education and increased in importance as voters and consumers.

The Kondratieff wave prior to the era of Mass Consumption, starting around 1830-50, was the Age of Steel, Electricity and Heavy Engineering. It appeared due to the invention of the Bessemer furnace that allowed steel to be produced of such high strength and quality that entirely new products could be created. The steel industry became the leading industry that defined the new economy although tremendous growth was also seen in railroads, iron, coal and chemicals, many of which were connected with steel innovations.

Steel made the railways, ships, machines, construction equipment, weapons and bridges that were the focus of industrialization at that time. Stronger steel rails made it possible for each train to carry heavier loads so that they became more efficient. With stronger railways being built, mass transport blossomed during this time because transportation costs were reduced by a factor of 200. Factory workers also became the largest occupational group in society, which lead to the formation of unions and socialist groups that dramatically changed culture. As with the automobile-petrochemical K-wave, this K-wave changed virtually all levels of society.

Prior to this Kondratieff wave was the Age of Steam triggered by the invention of the steam engine (~1770) and its application to the textile industry as the largest beneficiary. Textiles, especially cotton, became the leading, most prosperous industry that defined the new economy. At this time the production of fabrics, yarns and clothing shifted from home-based production to factory-based manufacturing, a revolutionary development made possible because of the new steam engines. This caused a mass migration of workers from the countryside to cities, which responded in turn by building new housing, streets, water systems and sewage systems. During this time factory workers arose as a new social class who started fighting for their political rights.

Typically a brand new type of expansive infrastructure develops as a byproduct of the innovation forces unleashed during a Kondratieff wave. For instance, the railroad network was developed in the Age of Steel born due to the invention of the Bessemer furnace, society everywhere became connected to electrical systems during the next K-wave, road and highway networks sprouted up across countries in the subsequent K-wave of the automobile, and global telecommunications networks have appeared everywhere in the present Kondratieff wave that is defined by computers, telecommunications and digital information.

The Kondratieff wave has been traced back in economic statistics and price series more than 1,000 years. For instance, Richard Mogey and others have found long waves in prices back to the 10th century. Michael Alexander (*The Kondratiev Cycle*) traced the leading economic sectors of K-waves back to the early 1500s by studying the S-shaped diffusion curves of the leading industries that enjoyed the K-wave benefits. Here is the typical pattern of progress.

First an innovation would appear and produce a new industry that developed as the result of the technological revolution. Then various revolutionary changes would take place in related economic sectors that subsequently became the leading sectors of the economy offering the best investor returns. Financial capital would be attracted to these new sectors of development, accelerating their hold on what became the new major force within the economy. After a period of great profits, penetrating diffusion and eventually diminishing returns, there would appear a time of crisis and stagnation followed by an entirely new K-wave of entirely different innovations and technological revolutions. During the downswing of any K-wave, various innovations were always quietly developing in the background that would stimulate the next upswing when adopted.

George Modelski and William Thompson (*Leading Sectors and World Powers*) traced K-waves all the way back to Sung dynasty China. They also confirmed the repetitive pattern that Kondratieff waves were characterized by revolutionary innovations such as the invention of woodblock printing and paper printing (that improved communications); the establishment of national sales markets and paper currency (that revolutionized economic networks and the transactions for buying and selling goods); fiscal governance reformations (that reduced economic taxes and inefficiencies); and naval and maritime trade expansion dependent upon the compass (that increased global trade networks).

When we analyze a number of Kondratieff waves and their impact on economic prosperity, their economic benefits can often be viewed as the result of *greater efficiencies they offered*. These efficiencies arose from a variety of alternatives such as new transport modes that cut transportation costs and times (canals, railroads, roads, bridges); new trade routes along with new products they made readily available; cheaper or faster communication and information flows (woodblock printing, telecommunications); more efficient and inexpensive sources of energy (steam and electricity); cheaper market clearing mechanisms (fairs and trade markets and reduced tax systems); cheaper production techniques (steam motors, mass production), or any other "cheaper" improvement that added value.

Kondratieff waves are basically innovation waves - long-term waves of technological process which produce economic progress because they increase the efficiencies of production by cutting costs and increasing trade. Thus they boost economies. Sometimes they constitute grand political innovations that bring peace or lower taxes and thereby create large economic efficiencies as well.

If we were to roughly map out the innovations or leading prosperity sectors that most characterized past Kondratieff waves it would look somewhat as follows:

World Power	Date	Innovation/Leading Sector
Northern Sung	930	Woodblock printing
	990	National market formed
Southern Sung	1060	Public finance reform
	1120	Maritime trade expansion
Genoa	1190	Champaigne fairs
	1250	Black Sea trade
Venice	1300	Galley fleets
	1350	Pepper trade & Spanish gold
Portugal	1420	Guinea gold
	1492	Spices
Dutch Republic	1540	Baltic trade
	1580	Asian trade
Britain	1640	American plantations (rum, tobacco, slaves)
	1680	Amerasian trade (tea, coffee, sugar)
	1740	Cotton, textiles
	1790	Railroads and industry
USA	1850	Steel, electric power, heavy engineering
	1914	Automobiles
	1973	Information technology & telecommunications

The countries which lead the others in developing or adopting to the basic innovation forces of a Kondratieff cycle usually flourished by becoming the most highly productive economies. They become leading powers due to their alignment with the forces of the K-wave. As a result of becoming a leading economic power they experienced the most prosperity, and then achieved a subsequent bonus of becoming able to finance the largest armies. This is how many nations were able to become the leading hegemons and superpowers of their day. It was all due to aligning with the reigning Kondratieff wave and modernizing quickest by adopting the latest technology and innovations. Companies that aligned with these trends also became wealthy.

You can easily visualize the world economy over time according to the Kondratieff theory of innovation waves that penetrate the world economy in approximately sixty year chunks. Remember that K-waves have a length that is variable rather than fixed at exactly sixty years. Some analysts have even suggested a pattern where the transfer of power from one world hegemon to another occurs during three consecutive Kondratieff long-wave cycles, which will take approximately 180 to 250 years to run through the normal pattern. Coincidentally, this roughly corresponds to Peter Turchin's finding that secular prosperity waves in agrarian societies are around 2-3 centuries long, and Glubb Pasha's experience that empires last on average around 250 years. Incidentally, Modelski and Thompson also noted that "Successive powers emerge as the leading nations of their time in roughly 150 year cycles."

During the first K-wave of this centuries long preeminence process, a current regional or world leader weakens and a new leader starts to emerge, sometimes becoming that leader through war. Near the end of this first K-wave, the new leader who has assumed the helm of preeminence experiences a depression as it starts to learn the ropes of being a superpower.

During a second K-wave, the new hegemon solidifies its position through trade and accumulates substantial wealth, political influence and power. It experiences a golden age of economic achievement unmatched by any other nation. It once again experiences a depression at the end of the Kondratieff boom when market saturation of the innovational forces finally takes place, the leading industries mature and investment returns in these sectors start to decline. However, this depression is lighter than the first one years ago because social safety nets and a bureaucracy have been established since that first K-wave and help to soften the blow. However, these social safety nets set the stage for excessive inflation, social spending and hegemonic decline during the third K-wave in the series.

In the third consecutive K-wave experienced by a world leader, there is less capital available for new innovations and industries than in previous waves since the increased social welfare spending has necessitated that money be extracted from productive private industry and its commercial development efforts. Inflation roars this time around and the economy experiences stagnant growth. Socialist movements sprout up while a new world leader is in the wings ready to emerge. This competitor does not have to shoulder many of the leader's social spending burdens, and is waiting to display its full feathers. Eventually socialism becomes so intense for the present world leader, with higher taxes impeding economic development, that it falls in rank from being the leading political and economic powerhouse. Shouldering excessive costs, it is then replaced by a new leader who has less social welfare spending, government debt, active military expenditures, regulatory burdens and other baggage.

A typical 60-year Kondratieff pattern can also be broken down into roughly five or six decades of expectations, with a decade being ten years or more. Here is a rough but typical pattern that describes these decades.

In the first decade a nation sees an economic recovery (from the final run-out of the old K-wave) characterized by a conservative social mood, modest speculative activities and protectionist foreign trade policies that help the economy.

In the second decade of its development, a Kondratieff wave nation often sees a period of wealth accumulation accompanied by war. Countries going through this portion of the cycle tend to maximize their wealth by free trade tendencies, but increasing levels of wealth often bring on arrogance and the tendency for war, which coalesces the nation. This is basically a stage of economic expansion where the nation may or may not militarize its wealth.

In the third decade of K-wave growth a nation will also experience prosperity and possibly war. The country will still engage in free trade and become involved in progressive, reform-minded legislation. However, the fourth decade is roughly one of transition and stagnation where a nation becomes internationalist and protectionist in its attitudes.

In the last decade the nation finally experiences a depression and decline characterized by deflation where extreme levels of debt built up during the ascendancy phase are now wiped out. The social mood at this time becomes dominated by conservatism and demands for extreme protectionism. Citizens emphasize their rights rather than duty to the nation. One might say that the economy, mired in debt, overextends itself before a decline begins, and then the asabiya of hard work and self-sacrifice disappears as the K-wave completes its cycle.

Investing that Aligns With K-waves

If one is managing generational wealth (such as a university endowment) you can think of the K-wave as a long-term investment cycle and should consider the best investment possibilities within its structural phases in order to maximize your wealth. A 60-year K-wave can be broken down into a cycle that resembles the four seasons of the year – a Spring, Summer, Autumn and Winter – each of which favors a different type of investment. While there are also different population behaviors in each phase of the economic cycle, the key principle is that phases of the K-wave give you a blueprint for where an economy stands and where it is headed. This is knowledge one should make use of for personal investments or for guiding a nation.

Each season of the Kondratieff wave has different economic, psychological and best investment characteristics (similar to what you find in Elliott wave explanations) and you can use these as an investment guide within the phases of the long wave structure. In other words, a strategy for maximizing your wealth in the long-run is to invest in different types of assets according to where you are (the phase) within a K-wave cycle.[15] You want assets that will do well in that particular type of environment.

During Spring time an economy starts refreshed after a K-wave Winter where the economy has died and excessive debt has been wiped out of the system. It is an expansionary time period characterized by benign inflation where new innovation sparks economic production and growth. There is inflationary growth while employment and consumer confidence start to once again steadily increase. The best investments during this time period are typically stocks and real estate that benefit from the economic green shoots.

During K-wave Summers an economy finally starts to fully bloom and bear fruit again. Business is thriving and stock prices and commodity prices boom. This period always tends to experience runaway inflation where you also typically see increasing debt loads due to loans to companies, soaring commodity and real estate prices, and overbuilding in the capital sector. In many cases there is a war during this period. For instance, the Untied States saw the War of 1812, Civil War, WWI and Vietnam War in this phase of its Kondratieff cycles. Kondratieff Summers are a time to profitably invest in commodities, gold and residential real estate because of the inflation bubble. Gold tends to prosper during periods of negative real interest rates. One has to be careful not to fall prey to arrogance, greed and optimism during this and the next phase of the Kondratieff cycle.

During K-wave Autumn periods we tend to see flat or disinflationary growth (early deflation) and recessions. Consumers still want to spend like they did during the Summer period, so they accumulate massive amounts of debt which reaches unsustainable levels. Stocks peak during this period and then they often crash. Investors become so enamored of their speculative success that they fail to see the bubble around them until it collapses. The economy sees decreasing commodity prices while debts build exponentially, rising to unsustainable levels. The Autumn phase of the K-wave cycle is therefore a time to favor investments in stocks (before they crash), bonds and commercial real estate. With judicious selection and timing, those can be the best performing assets during this phase.

During Winter periods of the cycle we normally see the death or destruction of an economy through debt defaults, deflations and depressions. You will typically see banking crises, corporate bankruptcies, debt repudiation, declining consumer confidence, rapidly falling prices, and

---

[15] If interested solely in asset switching strategies over the long-term for growing your wealth see *Super Investing: 5 Proven Methods for Beating the Market and Retiring Rich* by Bill Bodri.

high unemployment during this phase of the K-wave cycle. Investors should switch to defensive investments at this time by holding cash, gold and silver, and real assets that tend to hold their value during financial catastrophes. This phase lasts until the excessive debt is cleared out of the system and the "next big thing" comes along, which is the next new innovation wave.

Famed economist Joseph Schumpeter strongly felt that national economies moved in waves not just because of the longer-term Kondratieff wave by itself but as the result of four main cycles acting in tandem: the Kondratieff wave, Kuznets infrastructure investment cycle (15-25 years in length), Juglar fixed investment cycle (7-11 years on average) and Kitchen cycle (about 4 years).

International Asset Allocation and Investment Models

If you are managing a generational wealth fund, good asset allocation policies are necessary for the best buy-and-hold strategies meant to catch the plum parts of these waves (see *The Ivy Endowment* and *Global Asset Allocation* by Mebane Faber and *DIY Financial Advisor* by Wesley Gray). While there are really only two investment methods that will last over the long run – value investing and momentum investing – a smart investor can make deft investments in economic sectors, rotating asset allocations according to these phases.

The best asset allocation method I ever discovered was revealed in Mark Boucher's *The Hedge Fund Edge*. Within, Boucher tells the story of how he met a very private European money manager, with failing health, who after many years in the investment business decided to teach Mark his highly secretive method for managing billions for superior returns. This European manager had achieved an amazing long-term compound annual growth rate (CAGR) greater than 19% since the mid-1950's without ever having a drawdown greater than 20% on the funds he managed. Furthermore, in over thirty years of managing money he had only seen one negative calendar year (-5% in 1974)!

This outstanding asset allocation method concentrates on monitoring all the stock markets in the world and buying those that are currently advancing better than all others (as determined by a relative strength ranking), but only gets into those markets if there is a fundamental basis supporting those advancing moves. In other words, it practices a form of *momentum investing* by always buying just the world's best performing stock markets. You rotate into a country's stock market when it starts outperforming everybody else, and you get out of that market when it falls out of the top tier of outperformers. Before investing in some foreign stock market, however, there must be some *fundamental reason* (underlying monetary conditions) behind its upward advance involving interest rates, namely a favorable interest rate environment to support the bullish trend.

If a country's stock market was performing well—meaning it was above its 40-week moving average—the trend was assumed to continue as long as there were fundamental reasons behind the advance. Thus, the manager was looking to invest in world stock markets that were already moving up and which also had a favorable interest rate environment, which he monitored by looking at a 40-week moving average of the bond and treasury bill prices for each market. If a country's stock and bond markets did not have these two characteristics, he didn't even consider it as a possibility for investment. Anytime a country's stock index fell below its 40-week moving average, it was eliminated from consideration. Anytime the treasury bond and bill prices (the long rate and short rate) for a country both fell below their 40-week moving averages, he also eliminated that market from investment consideration because this meant that interest rate trends in that country were unfavorable.

Boucher said that he also kept a 6-month relative strength table of world stock market indices that compared as many global markets as possible. He additionally produced a 6-month relative strength table of world interest rate trends too. To analyze world interest rates he created a 6-month global relative strength table for all 10-year bond markets and all 90-day short rate prices, and then averaged the two indices together for each country to come up with a single composite number. If 10-year bond prices were going up for a country (if they were greater than their 40-week moving average) it was considered bullish because it meant interest rates were falling. If short-term interest rates were falling (if they were less than their 40-week moving average) it was considered bullish as well.

After constructing a relative strength table for all the world's stock markets and interest rate markets, the secretive international fund manager only considered investing in markets where both the stock market trend and the interest rate trend were favorable. He was basically sorting all the world's markets into an "A" pile and "B" pile. The "A" pile contained stock markets that were already going up where the interest rate environment was also favorable. The "B" pile contained markets where this wasn't happening, and so you wouldn't even consider those markets for investment. You were going to invest only in the "A" pile candidates and avoid the "B" pile markets because an upwards trend wasn't there or a positive monetary environment wasn't there either.

Thus, the asset allocation strategy was to invest only in some of the markets currently advancing if they also had strong interest rate fundamentals. You always avoided the "B" pile candidates since they had potentially negative consequences of "catastrophic risk." This money manager was not only looking for a positive momentum trend in each foreign stock market, and demanding that it be one of the best in the world, but was looking for confirmation via a favorable monetary environment in that country that could be spotted by interest rate trends – his "fundamentals."

By evaluating as many world markets as possible, this European manager could see who was doing better or worse than everyone else, and then position himself in several of the top markets. By always investing in the top tier of favorable stock markets, he was hedging his risks by practicing international diversification. By investing internationally, this also gave him the chance to outperform everyone else who was just limited to investing in their home nation. Perhaps, in a sense, he was capturing the sweet spots of K-waves or other economic prosperity waves within each country this way.

With his massive relative strength table finished, asset allocation was the final step. This manager simply took the top five markets from this list and put 20% of his money in each of those markets. If there were only four countries on the list, 25% of his investment funds would be allocated to each market equally. If there were only three countries on the list, 25% would go into each of the three markets, and 25% into T-bills or money markets to collect interest. If there were only two countries on the list, 25% would go into each of those two markets, and 50% would go into T-bills or money market funds. If there was only one country on the list, it would get 25% of his funds, and 75% would be put into T-bills or money markets.

If there were no countries with an advancing stock market and favorable interest rate environment, the funds would be parked in cash to collect interest until one or more advancing markets showed up. This allowed the manager to sidestep large drawdowns during bear markets. Finally, every six months, on January 1 and July 1, he would then rebalance his portfolio to include the new top-ranking countries from his table. If he found that a country had dropped off from his combo relative strength table, he would simply re-allocate those funds to another country that was now in the top tier of rankings. Which country? To one that had the highest rank of any he wasn't already invested in. This insured that he was always investing in countries that were experiencing the best performances due to interest rate fundamentals.

In most instances stock market investing can also be dramatically improved by relying on the twelve-year forward rate of return estimates, or ratio of equity market capitalization (non-financial equities) to corporate gross value-added (of non-financial companies included estimated foreign revenues), computed by investment manager John Hussman of Hussman Strategic Advisors. If you know that the projected stock market return over the next few years is negative, you will want to be out of the equity markets whereas if it is extremely positive you will want to be fully invested. The forward return projections are invaluable guides for long-term wealth investing and can be compared to historical returns from the secular studies performed by Ed Easterling (*Unexpected Returns*).

The 4-year Kitchen cycle noted by Schumpeter should be of particular interest to investors since four years also corresponds to the United States Presidential cycle. After years of research the famed value investor Benjamin Graham came up with a low P/E investment model that in my opinion adroitly made use of this 4-year cycle without Graham realizing it. Before he died Graham gave an interview published in the September 1976 issue of *Medical Economics* entitled, "Simplest Way to Select Bargain Stocks," where he explained this simplified technique that did away with all the complicated security analysis that he used to perform at the start of his career. He had become famous for this type of detailed analysis but surprisingly no longer used it.

Graham looked at twelve to thirteen factors to rate stocks at the beginning of his career, eventually cut it down to seven or eight factors, and finally to just two. He explained, "I have lost most of the interest I had in the details of security analysis which I devoted myself to so strenuously for so many years. I feel they are relatively unimportant, which, in a sense, has put me opposed to developments in the whole profession. I think we can do it successfully with a few techniques and simple principles."

His new model, excerpted from my book *Super Investing*, was as follows. First, create as large a list as possible of common stocks currently selling at no more than seven times their latest (not projected) 12-month earnings. While Graham said to select shares with a P/E of less than 7, he explained that he arrived at this criteria because he wanted an earnings-to-price ratio (the inverted P/E ratio) that was at least twice the average current yield on top-quality (AAA) corporate bonds. Today we might use a P/E criteria of 10 or even 12. In any case, the low P/E requirement tends to be the first sieve that helps you select underpriced stocks selling at a discount.

Once you have those initial candidates, you are looking to select a portfolio of at least 30 stocks (at a minimum) that not only meet the P/E requirements but also have strong balance sheets. You don't just want a low P/E but also want companies that are financially strong because they have a satisfactory financial position. Graham's only screening criteria for this condition was that a company should own at least twice what it owes, so its debt should be less than half of its assets. How do you measure this? You can look at the shareholder equity/total assets ratio to get an idea of debt levels. If you look at the ratio of stockholders' equity to total assets and the ratio is at least 50%, the company's financial condition can be considered sound.

Now for the selling rules. After you buy such a stock, you would sell it after it appreciated by 50% upwards or *after two years went by*, whichever came first, and then simply repeat the process when funds became available and new stocks meet the tests.

In other words, Graham would buy stocks (1) with an attractive low P/E ratio (meaning they were selling at a bargain) and (2) attractive shareholder equity/total assets ratio (so that if a company went bankrupt the financials were such that he could get his money back) and (3) a holding period for selling when the investment went up 50% or two years went by. *The two-year mark is half of the four-year investment (or Presidential) cycle!* If you happened to buy at an opportune time during this cycle because a stock was cheap relative to its true value, which would probably occur near its lows, you would also probably recover your money as the market traced back its two-year cyclical declines.

Fred Carach (see his interview in *Breakthrough Strategies of Wall Street Traders*) also came up with an interesting way to get rich by buying penny Canadian resource stocks when they reached five year lows, knowing that if their economics were cyclical he would probably be able to double or triple his money if he bought at that time and just held long enough.

Socionomics

Another cyclical factor to consider for its effect on regional economies are demographic issues, best taught by the economist Harry Dent. Each country has its own demographics, a specific composition of age groups, and as people grow older each age group exhibits specific spending patterns and economic effects that produce spending waves. For instance, in the United States peak consumer spending for individuals occurs near age 50 with the big spenders being 45 to 55 years old. A large increase in the numbers of this age group (given that there is no recession) will therefore provide a boost to a consumer-based economy.

Dent says that demographic climaxes in average peak spending led to the rising U.S. economic boom from 1983 to 2007. A slowdown started in 2008 that will carry on until 2020-23 when trends are expected to bottom out and then start turning up again. The demographic numbers and associated spending waves cannot predict individual stock market crashes and swings, but the big picture is undeniable.

Within these large demographic trends are also generational cycles, first described by William Strauss and Neil Howe in their books *Generations: The History of America's Future, 1584 to 2069* and *The Fourth Turning*. Strauss and Howe reveal a hidden asabiya of social trends creating history that is based on generations of people who possess a similar mindset.

The idea of a "generation" is that there is a common social type of thinking that affects a person's consciousness in the same way that class or culture does. Generational groups that think and act similarly are built through the influence of history on people's experiences and psyches. They are built from the effect of social events on the public in the sense that individuals of the same age group end up sharing similar value systems (basic attitudes towards family, risk, civic engagement, culture, etc.). Because of common influences on their lives, they tend to share a similar mindset and resemble their times more than their parents do.

To Strauss and Howe an average life lasts approximately eighty years and is composed of four stages each approximately twenty years long: childhood, young adult, midlife and elderhood. Thus a generation is an aggregate group of people born every twenty years or so such as Baby Boomers, Gen Xers, Millennials and Homelanders. Each generation goes through four "turnings" (highs and lows) every twenty years, namely a High period, Awakening period, Unraveling period and Crisis period. Each of these turnings also has a distinctive mood.

During a High period a nation's institutions are strong. Thus, social conformity is strong and individualism is weak. One might say asabiya is strong and focused on "We." During an Awakening period the mood is of cultural or religious renewal where institutions are attacked in the name of personal authenticity and spiritual autonomy. During an Unraveling period, institutions become weak/distrusted while individualism starts to flourish and people concentrate on enjoying themselves. Finally, the Crisis period is an era of destruction (often involving war or revolution) where institutional life is destroyed and then reorganized in response to a threat to national survival.

During the Crisis period some form of peril usually provokes a move toward societal consensus - the asabiya of "We" - and an ethic of personal sacrifice and institutional order. During Awakenings, on the other hand, the individualistic "I" ethic emerges wherein the established social order is attacked by new social ideas and spiritual agendas.

Strauss and Howe thus described four generations distinctly different from one another that tend to follow each other in sequence, each lasting around twenty years. In *Generational Dynamics*, John Xenakis charts out these generational impacts in the histories of Western Europe, Eastern Europe and Asia. The Strauss and Howe pattern is basically the same across countries: an Idealist generation is followed by a Reactive generation, followed by a Civic generation, followed by an Adaptive generation, and then the cycle begins all over again. Later Strauss and Howe changed these names to Prophet, Nomad, Hero, and Artist generations.

As a generation comes of age it defines its collective persona, which often happens while an opposing generational archetype is usually enjoying its own peak of power. This is reminiscent of how a new world leader/hegemon quietly becomes strong in the wings while a current leader is enjoying the spotlight.

A useful synopsis of Strauss and Howe's four major generational characters is as follows:

Prophet generations are born after a great war or other crisis, during a time of rejuvenated community life and consensus around a new societal order. Prophets grow up as the increasingly indulged children of this post-crisis era, come of age as narcissistic young crusaders of a spiritual awakening, cultivate principle as moralistic midlifers, and emerge as wise elders guiding another historical crisis. By virtue of this location in history, such generations tend to be remembered for their coming-of-age passion and their principled elder stewardship. Their principle endowments are often in the domain of vision, values, and religion. Their best-known historical leaders include John Winthrop, William Berkeley, Samuel Adams, Benjamin Franklin, James Polk, Abraham Lincoln, Herbert Hoover, and Franklin Roosevelt. These were principled moralists, summoners of human sacrifice, and wagers of righteous wars. Early in life, few saw combat in uniform; later in life, most came to be revered more for their inspiring words than for their grand deeds. (Example among today's living generations: Boomers.)

Nomad generations are born during a spiritual awakening, a time of social ideals and spiritual agendas when youth-fired attacks break out against the established institutional order. Nomads grow up as underprotected children during this awakening, come of age as alienated young adults in a post-awakening world, mellow into pragmatic midlife leaders during a historical crisis, and age into tough post-crisis elders. By virtue of this location in history, such generations tend to be remembered for their rising-adult years of hell-raising and for their midlife years of hands-on, get-it-done leadership. Their principle endowments are often in the domain of liberty, survival, and honor. Their best-known historical leaders include Nathaniel Bacon, William Stoughton, George Washington, John Adams, Ulysses Grant, Grover Cleveland, Harry Truman, and Dwight Eisenhower. These have been cunning, hard-to-fool realists—taciturn warriors who prefer to meet problems and adversaries one-on-one. (Example among today's living generations: Generation X.)

Hero generations are born after a spiritual awakening, during a time of individual pragmatism, self-reliance, laissez faire, and national (or sectional or ethnic) chauvinism. Heroes grow up as increasingly protected post-awakening children, come of age as the heroic young team-workers of a historical crisis, demonstrate hubris as energetic midlifers, and emerge as powerful elders attacked by another awakening. By virtue of this location in history, such generations tend to be remembered for their collective coming-of-age triumphs and their hubristic elder achievements. Their principle endowments are often in the domain of community, affluence, and technology. Their best-known historical leaders include Cotton Mather, "King" Carter, Thomas Jefferson, James Madison, John Kennedy, and Ronald Reagan. These have been vigorous and rational institution builders. In midlife, all have been aggressive advocates of economic prosperity and public optimism, and all have maintained a reputation for civic energy and competence to the very ends of their lives. (Examples among today's living generations: G.I.s and Millennials.)

Artist generations are born during a great war or other historical crisis, a time when great worldly perils boil off the complexity of life and public consensus, aggressive institutions, and personal sacrifice prevail. Artists grow up overprotected by adults preoccupied with the crisis, come of age as the sensitive young adults of a post-crisis world, break free as indecisive midlife leaders during a spiritual awakening, and age into empathic post-awakening elders. By virtue of this location in history, such generations tend to be remembered for their quiet years of rising adulthood and their midlife years of flexible, consensus-building leadership. Their principle endowments are often in the domain of pluralism, expertise and due process. Their best-known historical leaders include William Shirley, Cadwallader Colden, John Quincy Adams, Andrew Jackson, Theodore Roosevelt and Woodrow Wilson. These have been sensitive and complex social technicians, advocates of fair play and the politics of inclusion. (Examples among today's living generations: Silent and Homelanders.)[16]

Roy Williams and Michael Drew analyzed the Straus and Howe generational cycles in *Pendulum: How Past Generations Shape Our Present and Predict Our Future,* and divided them into more convenient "Me" versus "We" generations. They saw two generations of forty years each – "Me" and "We" - instead of four generations of twenty years each. However, the work of Strauss and Howe also tallies with their observation since Strauss and Howe classified the Idealist and Civic generations as dominant and the

---

[16] "Generational Archetypes," LifeCourse.com, accessed May 25, 2018, http://www.lifecourse.com/about/method/generational-archetypes.html).

Reactive and Adaptive generations as recessive. Dominant generations exhibit independent behavior and attitudes in defining an era, which is the "Me" ("I") generation, while Recessive generations play a dependent role in defining an era, which are "We" generations.

These ideas, which are derived from a study of American history, are reminiscent of Ibn Khaldun's ideas of asabiya ("We" generations) derived from Arab history and his hypothesis that a dynasty typically lasts four generations. The four generations time limit is based on the often noted observation that any large wealth accumulated in a family does not last more than three generations. The Chinese have a saying that encapsulates this at the level of families and individuals: "Three generations rich, fourth generation poor." Ibn Khaldun instructively noted,

It reaches its end in a single family within four successive generations ... The builder of the family's glory knows what it costs him to do the work, and he keeps the qualities that created his glory and made it last. The son who comes after him had personal contact with his father and thus learned those things from him. However, he is inferior to him in this respect, inasmuch as a person who learns things through study is inferior to a person who knows them from practical applications. The third generation must be content with imitation, and, in particular, reliance upon tradition. This member is inferior to him of the second generation, inasmuch as a person who relies upon tradition is inferior to a person who exercises independent judgment. The fourth generation, then, is inferior to the preceding ones in every respect ... He imagines that the edifice was not built through application and effort. He thinks that it is something due his people from the very beginning by virtue of the mere fact of their descent, and not something that resulted from group effort and individual qualities.[17]

Michael Alexander also extensively studied the Kondratieff wave as well as the social trends noted by Strauss and Howe. In *The Kondratiev Cycle* he constructed a table listing the peak and trough periods of the Strauss-Howe generational cycles versus Kondratieff waves, noting that their alignment was too good to be mere coincidence.

Alexander wrote, "[My tables] present evidence that Strauss and Howe, when looking at cycles of religion, generational nurture, politics and popular culture were seeing the same human dynamic Kondratiev saw when looking

---

[17] Sohail Inayatullah, *Understanding Sakar: The Indian Episteme Macrohistory and Transformative Knowledge*, (Brill, Leiden, 2002), p. 210.

at cycles of prices, interest rates, industrial production and other economic variables. The two cycles are different sides of the same coin. Oscillating social stress produced by the economic K-cycle helps create the social moment conditions that impact people differently depending on their age, producing the differing generational peer personalities as described by Strauss and Howe's model. The presence of certain generations (and absence of others) determines the kind of response to Kondratiev stress that will be shown during a particular K-S upwave/social movement turning. If the adult phases of life are dominated by generations having peer personalities of a less materialist nature (e.g. Adaptives and Idealist) the social moment will be a Spiritual Awakening. If the adult generations have materialist peer personalities (Civics and Reactives), the social moment will be a Secular Crisis."[18]

On top of all these patterns, for large scale insights into economic waves and generational patterns one can also turn to Elliott wave analysis (a form of financial analysis invented by Ralph Nelson Elliott, also known as EWT) and socionomics analysis (developed by Robert Prechter) to decode the linkages between a nation's stock market trends, economic strength, political movements, cultural trends and social mood.

Socionomics, which uses Elliott wave theory, decodes the social causality behind phenomena through the lens of stock market prices. It views the trend of stock market prices as a chart of rising (positive) and falling (negative) social mood; people buy stocks when their mood is positive and sell when it is negative. According to EWT and socionomics, it is not that rising prices lead to good moods and declining prices lead to negative moods. Rather, positive social mood usually leads to rising stock market prices, cheery social trends, upbeat entertainment themes, and peace and harmony between groups of people and nations. Negative social mood typically leads to falling stock markets, negative themes in popular entertainment, muted fashions, and conflict or war.

While most academics insist that events produce the mass psychology (social actions motivate social mood), such as the stock market gyrations themselves producing the net positive or negative social mood, Elliott wave theory and socionomics propose that it is the shared national social mood (its collective disposition or net emotional state) that produces those gyrations. The social mood (which harkens back to the ideas of asabiya and net generational characteristics) is the fundamental basis behind collective social events – social mood motivates social actions. According to EWT and socionomics, the national social mood is what influences actions by individuals and groups to create events and fashion history.

---

[18] Michael Alexander, *The Kondratiev Cycle: A Generational Interpretation*, (Writers Club Press, New York, 2002), pp. 131-132.

In other words, mass social psychology precedes actions; the primary influencer and shaper of history is the internal causality of social mood rather than the external causality of major events. Events appear within the dominant social mood; the mood creates the events. Therefore to guide a nation towards progress and prosperity you must learn to mange its social mood. You can reverse or stop social cycles only if you apply tremendous force the key is to instead *guide* the momentum of social forces to better outcomes.

While the standard view is that a war, political election and so forth will change the mood of a country, Elliott wave theory and socionomics sees it entirely different in that social mood is endogenous, destined to fluctuate according to known patterns, and is what produces those results rather than the other way around. The natural pattern of social moods is called the "wave principle" or "wave structure" of Elliott wave analysis.

While this sounds counterintuitive, socionomics would be able to tell you that the political environment is likely to turn dangerous whereas conventional social theory would have you trapped within Germany when its economy was improving but the Nazis were taking over. Similarly, conventional economics would have you fully invested and then losing everything during a major financial crash, whereas socionomics would tell you when and where to expect such destructive downswings. The stock market is the primary indicator of social mood that one can measure in a country, and the leading indicator of the economy. This is why macroeconomic results, for a fact, therefore lag the stock market.

Whatever you call all these repeated patterns, processes, trends, cycles or recurrent social forces, as a national leader or private investor you need to tap into and align with them in order to bring about progress and prosperity. A famous Chinese strategist Zhuge Liang once said, "When opportunities occur through events but you do not respond, then you are not smart. When opportunities become active through a trend but you do not formulate plans, then you are not wise. When opportunities emerge through conditions but you do not act on them, you are not bold enough."

Powerful possibilities open up when you understand the typical evolutions exposed by these and other frameworks. They allow you to align with the trend and bring prosperity to yourself and your country.

The Chinese sage Kuan Tzu said that making skillful use of timing is more beneficial than formulating strategies to bring about change because by taking advantage of timing you can achieve far more with less effort. Therefore you need to understand these forces and align with them to achieve maximum benefits.

5
CITIES

"It was the best of times, it was the worst of times, it was the age of wisdom, it was the age of foolishness, it was the epoch of belief, it was the epoch of incredulity, it was the season of Light, it was the season of Darkness, it was the spring of hope, it was the winter of despair, we had everything before us, we had nothing before us, we were all going direct to Heaven, we were all going direct the other way."
- *A Tale of Two Cities*, Charles Dickens

Every moment in the universe is just a neutral instant of time, an opportunity pregnant with the possibility that you will either move forwards or backwards. The direction you head, whether towards darkness or light, progress or decline, is all due to the decisions you make and where you move due to your energies and efforts.

When we look back upon the history of cultures, countries and empires to see those that have risen and those that have declined, one must admit that elevation or deterioration was not just due to external circumstances, but internally due to the wise or foolish decisions of the leaders as well as the temperament of the masses.

Those who run countries can guide them towards affluence, plentitude and abundance by aligning their policies with the best principles of prosperity and helping the people remain strong and unified, or through injudicious policies they can turn everything towards a road of destruction. This principle holds for cities as well.

In the pre-Christian era, the most populated cities in the world were names few would recognize, but in 1 AD the largest city on our globe was Rome. In 500 AD it was Constantinople. In 1000 AD it was Baghdad. In 1500 AD it was Beijing. The year 1900 saw London become the largest city in the world, and right now Tokyo and Sao Paulo are the largest (most populated) urban areas on the planet. The population leader has definitely changed over time.

If we were looking to see whether this type of variability happens within countries too, we need only turn to Tertius Chandler's *Four Thousand Years of Urban Growth* to note how the largest city in China dramatically changed over the years:

Ao (Cheng chow)	1360 BC
Anyang	1200 BC
Loyang	800 BC
Lintzu	650 BC
Yenhsiatu	430 BC
Chang-an	200 BC
Loyang	100 AD
Nanjing	361
Loyang	200
Chang-an	622
Chang-an	800
Chang-an	900
Kaifeng	1000
Kaifeng	1150
Hangzhou	1200
Nanjing	1400
Beijing	1500
Beijing	1700
Shanghai	1900
Shanghai	1925
Shanghai	1980

The simple conclusion we can draw from this short list is that superiority, leadership, hegemony, or preeminence is a characteristic of impermanence. No one stays the same forever. Cities suffer the same fate of ascendancy and decline as do empires, countries, cultures and civilizations. Even the largest city within a country right now might not even exist in the future. Plenty are the once great cities that are now graveyards of rubble under multiple layers of dust and dirt.

Cities can seemingly burst out of nowhere and expand in importance to displace other prominent centers of prosperity, and then decline into oblivion without leaving a trace. Like empires, countries, civilizations and religions, they go through natural rises and falls due to changing circumstances.

The great historian Herodotus wrote, "The cities that were formerly great have most of them become insignificant; and those which are presently powerful were weak in olden times. I shall therefore discourse equally on both, convinced that human happiness never continues long in one stay."

Since even cities with the greatest of advantages will lose their preeminence and disappear over time, in search of the wisdom to prevent this we should ask ourselves what are the most common reasons behind the fall of great cities?

The first reason is obvious – a very common cause of decline is the destruction caused by warfare or invasion, which in the past caused the downfall of famous cities such as Babylon, Carthage, Rome, and Angkor Wat in Cambodia. Wars bring destruction to cities, countries and empires, plain and simple. What may take generations to build can be destroyed overnight by a war or invasion.

An interesting lesson we might also derive from examining historical records, since it has happened so often, is that empires, countries and cities that grew rich through warfare also seem to suffer the karmic recompense of losing their own wealth and standing through warfare too. Hence the adage, "Get rich through warfare, lose all through warfare." If you determine to grow rich through military conquests to enlarge your realm and steal the wealth of others, this is a precarious policy that usually ends in your own destruction.

Historians have noted that rising empires tend to be judicious in their use of military force, but declining empires are prone to "wild swings of the bat" to maintain a top position. A related recent example is when Britain invaded Egypt in 1956 after the nationalization of the Suez Canal but had to retreat, thus triggering a financial crisis and the end of the British pound as the world's reserve currency. Britain's military foray marked the death of the British Empire.

Another reason a great city falls is when it owes its prosperity to being located along a trading route, and then an alternative trading route is developed to bypass it. Locational advantages are not eternal even though they might seem indestructible at the moment. For instance, the cities of Turfan, Khotan, Kashgar, Samarkand and Bactra were all centers of prosperity along the Silk Road, but lost their preeminence when the Portuguese opened a sea route to Asia at the end of the 15th century. The sophisticated Italian trading and financial cities of Venice, Amalfi and Genoa were also hit by tremendous downswings when Vasco da Gama circumnavigated the Cape of Good Hope in Africa, opening an entirely new trading route to the Orient in 1498. More recently the stagnation of Buffalo NY since the 1950s can be traced to the construction of the Saint Lawrence Seaway that allowed goods headed eastward to bypass Buffalo.

If a city primarily owes its prosperity to the lucky circumstance of being located along a trading route, it is sure to experience some degree of economic decline when competing routes are developed. Monterrey in Mexico, for instance, has grown because it is located near the Texas border on the main highway linking Mexico City with the United States. If an alternative highway gains popularity then Monterrey's economy will suffer. Furthermore, when cities like Monterrey are the satellites of an imperial regime they can also lose their protection if their home state is attacked, thus their survival will be at risk under these conditions as well.

Lao Tzu once said that small countries must survive by humbly serving their powerful neighbors. Cities located on the edge of a huge empire, which fit this characteristic, may often benefit through a parasitic or servant derived type of prosperity, but are also militarily vulnerable to the larger nation from which they feed. Less powerful than their neighbor, to survive their neighbor's expansionist ambitions requires that they develop their own counterbalancing protections just as Qatar, Jordan and the UAE have done due to their proximity to Saudi Arabia. Furthermore, such countries or cities must also diversify their economies away from becoming too dependent on their powerful neighbor.

The lesson from history is that a city's location will help to determine its prosperity and what types of economic activities are likely to succeed in that locale. Certain cities are more attractive than others for special economic activities simply because of their locations and the circumstances or opportunities this provides, such as easy access to raw materials, transportation routes, regulatory environment, an educated or skilled populace, or low labor costs. Manufacturing jobs, for instance, do not just flow to countries or cities with the lowest labor costs. The primary considerations companies use when deciding to locate in a region include the availability of skilled labor, the presence or not of the rule of law, regulations, the tax rate, and the social taxable contributions required on labor. Many times companies will turn down lucrative business opportunities in locations that simply lack the rule of law, showing that political risk is just as important as cost concerns. In light of the new global economy, cities and countries that want to attract businesses must be competitive not just on labor costs but on their total taxation and regulation costs too. Companies tend to relocate to where regulation is the least intrusive and taxation the most favorable.

Cities can also die due to a lack of economic diversification, a perfect example being the deterioration of Detroit MI because of the decline in automobile manufacturing. A city might grow rich through boom time production of a particular key commodity or industry, such as silver or rubber or auto production, but will go from riches to poverty when its specialization is no longer needed by the world markets, or when others can supply their products cheaper. If they experience competitors, such as when China's monopoly on tea was broken by tea plantations created in Ceylon, Kenya, and Turkey, their economies are sure to suffer.

When Robert Fortune stole tea from China so that it could be grown elsewhere it was one of the greatest thefts of protected trade secrets that the world has ever known, so the "comparative advantage" touted for nations and cities never lasts. Another theft that hurt China's economy was when its highly protected silkworm eggs were smuggled out of the country, thus enabling silk production competitors to spring up in quite a few other nations. Locational advantages, trade secrets and technological preeminence never last forever.

If markets become saturated with a city's main product, if city production costs rise over competitors' costs, if a city's productivity declines, if substitutes for products especially produced within a city are developed, the natural resources in a region are used up, … these are all examples of circumstances that can also lead to a city's demise regardless of whether it is a commodity producer or industrial powerhouse.

When demand drops for the small number of products or services a city produces that brought it its riches, or when its main industry goes into decline, its prosperity almost always suffers a downturn. This is why cities must always strive to diversify their economies away from acute specialization as much as possible. When dependent upon a single commodity their economic fortunes can easily weaken and their importance can be displaced by any more efficient newcomer.

A prosperous city that remains prosperous is typically one whose economy exhibits *complexity in income* – a wide variety of independent revenues due to a wide collection of industries. With a wide variety of talent at its disposal, this type of city has the best chances of staying strong or reinventing itself when circumstances change.

Rich cities are like countries, companies and even leaders who can at times turn overconfident. Whether it is due to an excess of arrogance and hubris or just plain stupidity, they sometimes end up trying to over-expand beyond their means and expertise, venturing into areas they don't understand, and then overspend from overstretching themselves. After they become heady with the success of prosperity they often bring their own downfall upon themselves by engaging in aggressive, expansionist overstretch efforts that fail, such as Napoleon's catastrophic advance into Russia. Some take on incredible debts that cannot be paid, while others gut their own productive industries to instead import luxuries produced by others, thus producing insurmountable trade deficits. Spain chose this course of action that caused it to lose its supremacy status in the 1500s, and when the U.S. started outsourcing its manufacturing industries it chose this same route of destruction as well.

The Spanish story is quite instructive for the lessons it reveals. In just over one hundred years, sixteenth century Hapsburg Spain went from being a near nothing nation to becoming a great empire, and then destroyed itself to become a nothing nation once again. The conquered gold and silver riches of Mexico, Central America and South American flowed into Spain, slowly dis-incentivizing national production and turning the nation into a consumption-based economy which imported opulent goods from all over the world rather than manufacture them. Government expenditures soon exceeded income, thus setting the stage for decline.

Because of its growing wealth, with arrogance Spain began to think of itself as supreme over all other nations, and started waging countless wars with other countries due to hubris. However, it ran out of funds, flirted with bankruptcy, and eventually had to borrow money to stay afloat since much of its gold and silver had left the country to buy imports or been lost through military misadventure. Spain had already stopped producing many products on its own in favor of imports, so this decline was inevitable. The fall of Spain was associated with a fiscal crisis where government expenditures eventually exceeded revenues and where the mounting costs of servicing government debt became impossible to pay.

As stated, this pattern has consistently been associated with many imperial declines, and it happens for cities too. In 1543 nearly two-thirds of Spanish ordinary revenues were used for interest payments on government borrowings, and by 1598 the monarchy had to spend 100% of revenues just to service its debt, which essentially led to the country's collapse. The case of Spain reveals a consistent pattern of history that also happens to cities that take on too many social welfare obligations and too much debt, and then lose their competitive economy.

As Michael Maloney warned, many countries run into monetary troubles and then debase their currencies to produce inflation and poverty. Ancient cities that issued their own currency also encountered these troubles. Another route of decline is that they often got involved in foreign markets they didn't understand – a perfect example being Rome's many attempts to acquire new territories to bring in more revenues, whereas it often failed to make profitable acquisitions.

Some cities grow rich by establishing themselves as a banking center (or tax haven) that services trade, but without other advantages these eventually fall into peril because of their specialization. Marc Faber (*Riding the Millennial Storm*) noted, "Financial centers simply do not control their own destiny.

They are controlled by their debtors. Without a powerful military, they can, in the worst case, never enforce their claims." London, a financial center that doesn't make anything, needs to remember this warning.

What Makes a City Great

As opposed to decline, the other question arises as to what factors tend to make a city great. In the past, almost as a requirement the great cities tended to develop along waterways that could make agricultural lands fertile through irrigation. Waterways not only made ample food supply possible but also served as an essential transportation conduit for trade. Furthermore, the ready access to clean water helped to solve sanitation and hygiene issues, thus leading to improved health conditions that typically taxed cities as they grew larger. For instance, until London put in its own famous sewerage system the River Thames was an open sewer, the city smelled like crap, and Londoners constantly suffered from epidemics and other disease consequences.

Resource-riches other than agriculture have also helped to build many cities to greatness, and in more recent times a predominance of low cost workers or educated professionals, public access to higher education, an emphasis on technology development and a host of other factors have become responsible for urban prosperity.

The shift from agriculture to manufacturing over the ages has solidified the observation that the wealth of a nation develops within its cities and their surrounding urban environment, and then percolates to the top. Cities are the drivers of wealth, not nations. Nations simply aggregate the wealth produced by cities and men. Entrepreneurs within cities conduct banking, trade and work (by themselves or through companies they form) on a local level to crate or replace imported goods with locally produced alternatives, leading to vibrant growth, and it is their innovations that become the center of economics. To empower this type of inventive innovation a city must attract brains and talent that will flock to it by fleeing less successful locales.

For a city to become one of the predominant centers within its nation or the world, history shows there are a few requirements that can help it gain the necessary advantages:

- The city should be a transportation hub that makes national and international trade easy; accessible, well-connected cities exhibit higher growth. Today the transportation hub requirement means that a city must have access to a modern airport, railway and road system and ports. In ancient times connectivity meant being a coastal city or being located next to a navigable river. Navigable waterways enable goods to be quickly and economically transported throughout a country, which is a key component to prosperity. New transportation technology and infrastructure can alter a city's locational advantages. One such example is the construction of the Erie Canal in the 1840s which thereby gave New York City access to western markets, thus solidifying its position as America's largest center.

- The city should be efficiently managed by good administrators who do not shy away from long-term commitments (note Hong Kong and Singapore). Culture and political-private leadership both play a role in the growth and prosperity of cities aspiring for excellence because they are responsible for their policy frameworks and governance. Because of differences in mindset, one type of leader might emphasize raising city exports whereas another might ask what it would take to make the region's industries become world class. Cities with a reputation for poor governance, corruption, violence or sub-standard institutions face an uphill battle for prosperity. A city aimed at prosperity must present itself as legally and economically fair to all participants and be administered according to a clear and impartial set of laws. Virgil reminds us in the *Aeneid* that the great art of the Roman Empire was, "To govern the people with authority and establish peace under the rule of law." The impartial rule of law (and fair taxation system) insures that one's assets are not stolen by the government, competitors or elites, who historically tend to oppress weaker parties that cannot protect themselves. Without a dependable legal system a city will not see strong capital formation and economic development. Without the rule of law, few will risk there capital to go there.

- Minorities should be given equal opportunity to excel, and given access to a level playing field of opportunities and law enforcement. Minority groups are often the ones who drive prosperity into new regions, so governance should not be set up in such a way that minorities fear they might be oppressed, thrown out or trampled upon. When there are no social welfare nets it has historically been immigrants, freed from the restrictions of their home towns and countries, who have been the most capitalistically motivated to make lives for themselves in foreign locales. When a city is dependent upon foreign trade, they have often increased the prosperity of their new home cities the most.

- A city should be politically tolerant of dissent where intellectuals offering new ideas, scientists making discoveries, and philosophers challenging tradition are not persecuted, imprisoned, tortured or killed. These are the individuals who help us drive society forward to make progress.

- Some cities can grow prominent if they become military powers, such as the Phoenician cities of Byblos, Sidon and Tyre or the Italian trading cities of Genoa, Amalfi, Florence, Pisa, and Venice. The Hanseatic League is also an example of a group of cities that became great not just because of economics but because they were part of a military collective that protected their commerce.
- A city should invest in good institutions and infrastructure including roads, bridges, canals and sewage systems. Adequate transportation systems lead to trade, trade leads to more commerce, and more commerce leads to economic prosperity. Schools are needed to educate the young; the sick and elderly require hospitals for medical care; and the middle aged require economic opportunities and jobs. Those cities that have lasted for centuries achieved longevity because they developed good legal frameworks, business/commercial and institutional infrastructure, strong administrative skills, military power and offered educational opportunities for the populace. They made themselves great places to live.

To survive, it is commonsense that all cities need access to clean water and food, and must have adequate infrastructure to deal with sewage and garbage. War is to be avoided, hygiene and clean water to be maintained, and food made readily available through access to open markets. As stated, schools are needed for the children, hospitals for the sick and elderly, and opportunities for entrepreneurs and the commons. Farming (agricultural), production (manufacturing) and trade are encouraged.

Historically the key to more recent growth has not so much been to make the elites rich but to create an opportune environment that would attract the young, ambitious and talented due to the great living conditions and opportunities provided. The talented and hardworking are the ones who make a city wealthy. When the people become rich then the city becomes rich and when cities become rich then their nation becomes rich. The key is to "store the wealth among the people" rather than store it with the elites, and to make sure that any wealth inequalities between the strata of society do not become too great. Great imbalances and inequalities often lead to revolutions that topple governments.

Lastly, a city should strive to grow a complex economy rather than predominantly rely on just a few particular industries or commodities. Just as Ireland was crippled during the Great Potato Famine because 40% of the population relied on just one crop, cities that do not diversify their economies subject themselves to a high risk of ruin. Through overdependence they put their very survival at risk.

City Branding and Placemaking

A city that aligns itself with particular values will channel its growth in special directions. In that way it can build not just its economy, but create magnetic placemaking attributes that will make it feel like a special place to visit, live, or do business. It can brand itself by what it chooses to align with, and that choice will color its culture and character.

For example, Atlantic City is known for gambling, Indianapolis for auto racing, New Orleans is associated with Dixieland jazz, Williamsburg VA is associated with colonial architecture, Silicon Valley is associated with technology startups, and Miami Beach is associated with beaches and nightlife. These associations may or may not "fit" people, so it is up to a city's leaders as to what type of environment, reputation and branding they might choose to build for the residents. Huntington Beach CA, for instance, is known as "Surf City USA," which also attracts a certain type of resident.

Today cities commonly attract investment not just because of their local economies, infrastructure, labor pools and services, but because of their efforts at placemaking, which is to build great communities with a branding or destination promise that is attractive and rewarding for businesses, residents and visitors. Placemaking attracts and anchors talent in place, and that lures companies to relocate to those locations or to locally arise. With companies come new jobs and revenue that can be taxed.

Cities must engage in placemaking since talent today is highly mobile. Talented workers have choices where they can live and in today's age they tend to search for a high quality of life. They typically choose to live in places with attractive urban communities. An attractive locale, as defined by several measures, draws talent into living and working there.

Many places within cities, for instance, attract talent, large companies and small business better than others because they are known for a certain atmosphere or special character such as a lively street life, cosmopolitanism, diversity, or a tradition of small businesses and entrepreneurial activity. Sustainable long-term economic growth most often tends to be local and home grown rather than imported because of the specific cultural and entrepreneurial environment promoted within a city. The principle is that if a city can design itself in a certain way (which includes fewer taxes and regulatory hurdles) it can then attract more residents or local businesses to sprout up. The question is the mixture of incentives to make this happen and how to attractively shape the city as it grows.

This gives rise to the need for cities to engage in "destination branding" along with placemaking to attract residents and companies. A city's branding is something that its managers and community leaders can develop over time. The "destination brand" of a city is like a unique selling proposition for what individuals, families or companies can expect from visiting or relocating to that locale. It must be founded upon distinctive, attractive qualities (benefits or advantages) that both residents and outsiders both recognize and desire.

You must think of a "city brand" as the enduring *essence* of the place that can be promoted to others as the gist of the locale, and it is one of the primary reasons for relocating there. It is a distinctive identity that reflects the city's core reality rather than just a collection of empty slogans that project a false propaganda.

A city represented as its true self, when seen in the best light, is always far better than projecting any type of empty propaganda. A city brand should constitute the core essence of what a city is made of and known for - the totality of thoughts, feelings, and expectations that people hold about the location ... both its reality and reputation. It should represent the city's "virtue" or "value." You can actively build this brand into something better over time.

A city's branding and reputation are derived not just from its facilities, institutions, infrastructure and governance, but especially from the culture, character and behavior of its residents. There are certain values or principles - such as friendliness, forward thinking, volunteerism, wellness, environmental stewardship, the culinary food, an emphasis on education, etcetera - that a city's residents tend to commonly subscribe to and live by that becomes the city's character and culture over time.

There are values by which residents grow their city's nature and the reason why a community becomes the way it is. The Romans called this the community's *virtus*, or character. The values of families become the values of communities and the values of its communities become the values of a nation. A city's branding differentiates it from other locations because it captures the core essence of this cultural character and succinctly represents its distinctive promise of value to residents and visitors.

The lesson in all this is that just as national leaders can actually carefully align with the principles of a grand strategy to bring about growth and prosperity, city officials and residents can do the same. They can actively build a city according to a strategic development and destination plan. They can consciously choose to build a more positive city atmosphere over time by especially encouraging small business growth, which creates the most jobs, and make it more attractive and livable.

Great empires, nations, cities and even companies rise and fall because of human decisions. Their fate is often due to the judicious or injudicious decisions of their leaders. As the great American historian Rufus Fears suggested, the leaders qualified to build great countries or cities and move them forward must possess four critical qualities:

- A bedrock of principles and fundamental truths they hold to
- A moral compass, or sense of right and wrong
- A vision of what the people and place can become, and
- The ability to build a consensus to achieve that vision.

Abraham Lincoln and Pericles of Athens are two examples who come to mind of men who fit those qualifications. Good leaders find a way to transcend a city's or country's many differences and appeal to a common theme, calling people to participate in core activities that define citizenship (group membership). They try to strengthen families rather than destroy families, recognizing that the stronger the bonds to our families then the stronger the cohesion of greater society, whether in the city or state. Strong families build strong cities, so they pursue and promote policies that strengthen and support the family ideal, "the first society," rather than work to undermine or redefine that ideal into something weaker. This is what builds strong communities and lessens social problems in total.

The city character building activities of placemaking requires leaders who can judiciously select policies and value alignments to auspiciously shape the community for happiness prosperity. Because this is so extremely important to a city, only individuals having the four leadership qualities, rather than those who are just pursuing power, money, fame or position, should be entrusted with such responsibilities.

6
COMPANIES

"Align with the ideal of providing better value and service to customers. If that cannot generate profit then what will? It is meritorious to satisfy customer desires in a better way than others and thereby lift the playing field to a higher standard of excellence."

Today the Dow Jones Industrial Average is composed from the prices of thirty company stocks, but when it was started in 1896 it consisted of only twelve companies. Those twelve companies might seem stodgy to us today but they were the greatest industrial leaders of their age. Let's look at these leading companies of that era and examine their ultimate fates.

The American Cotton Oil Company became part of Unilever and was dropped from the Dow in 1901. The American Sugar Company was acquired by another firm and dropped from the Dow in 1930. The American Tobacco Company was ordered by the Supreme Court to dissolve and then split into many smaller companies, being dropped from the Dow in 1985. The Chicago Gas Company was acquired by another company ten years later and was dropped from the Dow in 1915. General Electric has been in and out of the Dow Jones Industrial Average since its inception and was just recently replaced by Walgreens Boot Alliance in June 2018. Distilling & Cattle Feeding Company has evolved into Millennium Chemicals; the original company was dropped from the Dow in 1899. The Laclede Gas Company has become Spire Energy, but was dropped from the Dow in 1899. The National Lead Company is now called NL Industries and was dropped from the Dow in 1916. The North American Company was broken up by the SEC in 1946, and dropped from the Dow prior to that in 1930. Tennessee Coal, Iron and Railroad Company merged with its main competitor, U.S. Steel, in 1907, which is the year it was dropped from the Dow. The U.S. Leather Company was dropped from the Dow in 1928 and liquidated in 1952. Finally, the United States Rubber Company was acquired in 1990 by another company and dropped from the Dow Jones Industrial Average in 1928.

What can we learn from this short history of industrial powerhouses? The same lesson that applies everywhere: "God has not granted the boon of perpetuity to anyone or anything." We learned that none of these once preeminent companies had the staying power to remain dominant for more than a few years, which is the universal principle of impermanence. The strongest companies of their day suffered various fates of demise such as bankruptcy, dissolution, mergers, takeovers or simply delistings. To survive and thrive, you cannot remain inflexible but have to master adaptiveness.

You would have gone broke as a "buy and hold" investor if you just bought these great names at the beginning of the Dow Jones Average and closed your eyes hoping for the best. Like civilizations, cultures, empires and countries, no company is granted the blessing of supremacy forever. In fact, the components of the Dow Jones Average have changed 51 times since its inception. Old leaders drop out and new ones always come along to replace the old. You must be ever vigilant with your investment funds and not park your money with a stalwart whom you think will grow forever.

Why Companies Fail

Roughly 80% of new businesses survive past their first year of operations, meaning that 20% of new businesses fail in their first year. Normally about 70% will survive their second year in business. Within five years about half of new businesses will have failed, and only about 30% of companies will survive until their tenth year in business. Even for those who become established past a decade, once they pass some major operational hurdles and reach a certain size they tend to become arrogant and stop listening to their customers, or they frequently stop innovating to keep up with market desires. These faults often seal the fate of demise.

Some companies fail due to undercapitalization, others due to cash flow problems (uncontrolled growth can cause this), some due to poor management or incompetent employees, others due to competition being better than themselves, and sometimes failure is due to being a "me, too" business that has no special distinction or competitive advantage or over others. Many times business failure is due to the complacency of not being responsive to customers, thus causing them to leave and become customers of competitors. Sometimes it is simply due to poor sales and marketing.

Quite often companies fail because they fall into a "marketing myopia," which is where they focus on their products so much that they forget their overall business mission. An example is Eastman Kodak, which lost much of its sales to digital cameras because the executives did not realize that its business was photography rather than film. There is no such thing as a boon of perpetuity for products or businesses, so there is no such thing as a product that will last forever.

Theodore Levitt wrote a famous paper on this problem of marketing myopia where companies produced themselves into oblivion by continuing to nearsightedly focus on just selling their products/services rather than seeing the bigger picture of what business they were truly in and ignoring what consumers ultimately wanted. On the other hand, the reason that large companies like Corning and Dupont have survived over many decades is because they put a high priority on product research for innovations and were thoroughly customer-oriented about their true business.

Levitt pointed out that the railroad industry fell into decline because its executives assumed they were in the railroad business rather than the transportation business. The railroad companies became railroad-oriented rather than transportation-oriented. They became product-oriented rather than customer-oriented. They failed to answer the all important question, "What business are we really in?" Had its executives had the proper aim and realized that *they were in the transportation business rather than railroad business* they could have made moves that allowed them to continue to grow. To survive a company needs the merit of serving the public, and the railroads lost their way because they became focused on the wrong mission – railroads rather than transportation service. Another example is that of carburetors. When carburetor companies focused on producing the best, lowest-cost and highest quality automobile carburetor on the market, it didn't help when fuel injection came along and replaced it. A carburetor company's aim, or constancy of purpose, should have been on putting a mixture of fuel and air in an engine's combustion chamber and innovating something new and effective along those lines. If you don't think in this way, you might be optimizing a product whose life cycle was coming to an end.

Many companies make this mistake of overly focusing on their products and concentrating on the product attributes rather than what customers ultimately want. In time, most products can and will be replaced by competitive alternatives, and those replacements will be either products they make themselves or items produced by competitors old and new.

During the go-go years, however, many companies end up believing they will grow forever and presume a longevity to their firm and products due to a present unchallenged superiority or current lack of effective substitutes for their wares. They become blind to the vagaries of fate due to steadily growing sales and slowly lose sight of serving their customers because they end up focusing on the wrong company purpose, which ultimately leads to their decline. Their growth is often thwarted not because of market saturation but because of management failures. You have to keep the company focused on serving customer/market needs in an ever better fashion. You have to be focused on innovation. No sutomers ever asked for the electric light, telephone, or copy machine. Innovations come from the producers, and that must be you!

A company must be profitable, but in the best of all worlds it must have a mission that it fulfills in a profitable way - in a way that makes the mission profitable. If a company simply runs after profits without the guiding principles of a mission it often ends up running down the wrong roads to make money for money's sake, which is the sort of mistake that often leads to demise. For instance, at one time Merck was primarily governed by the philosophy of George Merck to manufacture "medicine for the people … not for profits" and was comfortably profitable. When it switched to the philosophy of being totally "focused on growth" under CEO Ray Gilmartin, it ran into financial difficulties due to "ethical troubles" with Vioxx.

Merck is a perfect example of a company that added extraordinary value and earned lots of money when it was pursuing a service mission but ran into trouble when it started simply pursuing profits. At some point in its development nearly every business can be considered a growth business based on the increasing sales of its products, but in many cases businesses fail due to a loss of vision such as this. For purposes of growth and to stay out of trouble, companies need to seek a fundamental reason for existence to guide the firm beyond just making money. Companies need to be willing to change everything about themselves except their highest core beliefs, principles and philosophy of doing business.

The Adizes Company Life Cycle

Sometimes we can trace a business's failure to the common problems that typically plague businesses at regular, identifiable junctures within an expected company life cycle. Just as empires and countries have typical life cycle patterns, companies do as well.

One of the world's experts of company life cycle characteristics and challenges at specific periods in their growth is management expert Ichak Adizes. His observations on the different types of professional management needed at life cycle junctures is instructive for understanding just how to manage firms at different stages in their development. Just as countries, cities and empires must be managed differently at different stages of their development, companies must be handled differently as well according to the stage of their maturity and problems hey face.

The commitment to building a company (or some sort of organization) usually starts with someone falling in love with an idea. At this initial start-up stage of Courtship with an idea, Adizes said that business founders focus on ideas and possibilities for products, and dream of plans without yet making a commitment. They make a lot of noise on what they might do or want to do - like an airplane ready to take off - until they finally commit by undertaking the risk. A need is identified in the marketplace, they respond to the need by developing a new product or service, a business is founded to do something and the founders and owners plunge in with great gusto. It all starts with a vision that starts propelling the company forward with full force.

After it is finally founded, in the Infancy stage of a new business the main issue becomes that of survival. The company's focus shifts from playing with creative ideas to getting results that can be sold. Cash becomes king, and the need to make sales to bring in cash to prevent bankruptcy drives everything. Nobody at this stage pays much attention to paperwork, controls, systems or policies because the focus is on getting things done. The founders at this stage typically work on trying to do everything themselves without delegating. The main risks at this stage are that the founders will lose control or the company will crash due to liquidity problems because of undercapitalization, poor sales, and poor cash flow management.

The next stage of development, or Go-go phase, is a rapid growth phase where sales are great, cash flow is positive, and the company starts to really take off. Profits increase and some limitations are relaxed so the founders begin to believe they are geniuses who can do no wrong. With rising enthusiasm due to success they have a hard time controlling themselves as they start seeing "opportunities everywhere." Due to bad judgment they often fall into trouble because of overextension moves made due to hubris and arrogance. At this stage a company is typically organized around people rather than functions. One of the big mortality risks at this stage is that other founder family members come into the organization and drive it into the ground because of their lack of skills and competence.

In the next stage of Adolescence, Adizes says a company takes on a new shape as it hires professional managers to systemize its administration. The new guys come in to fix the fact that there are no clear internal structures or responsibilities. They start to fix the problems of poor cost accounting, poor information flows, and a messy reward system for sales and staff. An attitude problem of "old-timers" vs. "new guys" usually now arises and starts to create internal conflicts until the founders and employees develop a unity of understanding and begin to feel they can work together. People have little time to serve customers at this stage and so many fixes are going on that the business often suffers from a temporary loss of vision and direction. It looks too inward rather than outward.

The next stage of development, called Prime, is when the company develops a renewed clarity of vision focused on growth. Also, the company now turns inward and really gets organized. It starts to focus on both sales *and* profits and establishes a fair balance between control and flexibility. It works on building a stable core upon which it can scale up and grow. Growth becomes the name of the game! The business soon experiences the benefits from reaching the optimum place on the product life-cycle curve.

In the next stage called Stability, the company is now strong and mature but is lacking, a degree of its early eagerness and aggressiveness. New ideas are welcomed but with less excitement than in previous times because there has been an internal shift that is now protecting the status quo. Financial controls are established which emphasize short-term results that inhibit long-term innovation. The internal emphasis on marketing and R&D wanes, which are the two fundamental pillars of a business.

The company has now matured and so in the subsequent stage of Aristocracy the company becomes focused on ROI (return on investment) as its measure of success. In this stage of maturity, what becomes important to the managers is their own status (exhibited by office size and décor, titles, etc.) rather than the success of the business, which they deem is an assured phenomenon on automatic. The internal business culture then starts emphasizing *how* things are done over *what* is being done and *why*. No one wants to make waves and so big initiatives (that might propel the company ahead) are avoided. Instead of incubating start-up ideas and innovations the now stodgy company starts acquiring other businesses instead in order to grow. To keep the company going its executives rely on the past rather than blaze new trails of innovation for the future.

In the Early Bureaucracy stage, which comes next, the company starts experiencing decay and a witch hunt begins to find out who did what wrong. It stumbles a bit trying to determine how to fix things. There are systemic diminishing returns, so cost reduction starts to take precedence over both marketing and new innovation efforts to increase revenues. Individuals inside the company start focusing on personal jealousies and the issue of survival. Corporate infighting and backstabbing proliferate where executives fight to protect their own turf.

In the next stage of Bureaucracy, if the company hasn't died by now it becomes extremely bureaucratic, ruled entirely by both external and internal politics. Paperwork abounds, manuals thicken, and rules and policies choke the final remains of creativity and innovation. Basically the company becomes static, like a mature AT&T.

In the final stage of Death, which is the logical conclusion that everyone could see coming, the company goes bankrupt. Whether slowly or suddenly it can no longer generate the cash it needs to survive, and death finally ensues.

Great Companies

Peter Drucker once said, "Because its purpose is to create a customer, business has two functions and only two functions. Marketing and Innovation. Marketing and innovation produces results … all the rest is costs." As seen, without a constant focus on innovation (new products or services, inventions, R&D, new markets, etc.) companies eventually stagnate and die. If they don't focus on cost effective marketing, this often contributes to decline as well because without it they won't be able to profitably sell their products and services.

For R&D innovation efforts (which are the basis of Kondratieff waves) I like companies to investigate TRIZ, the science of inventing, and for marketing strategy I like them to check into the many published books of Al Ries and Jack Trout, David Ogilvy, Jay Abraham, Dan Kennedy, Claude Hopkins and other marketing legends.

When you ask business leaders about the characteristics of "great companies" they will typically say that they are premier in their industry, widely acknowledged as "best" by knowledgeable business people, make a lasting impression on the world, and usually have lived enough time that they have proven themselves by passing through multiple products and life cycles. Somehow they developed a system, perhaps unique or perhaps not, that keeps them relevant and profitable at producing products and services that people want.

Most every company, however, must at sometime pass away because of the law of impermanence, which is what we saw in the history of many Dow Jones great ones. To avoid premature death, however, a company needs a commitment to greatness and growth (which includes sales and profitability) and a way to get there. It needs to adapt to survive. The British East India Company is often believed to be the most powerful corporation the world has ever seen, and history suggests that its profits, powers and longevity were due to its ability to adapt and keep pace with change.

There are all sorts of ingredients bandied about as the recipe to greatness, but I want to stress the principle that great companies are built by *ordinary people* who produce extraordinary, superb results because of a dedication to making everything they touch the best it can be. They take the goal of building an enduring company onto themselves, and then figure out what that entails in their particular circumstances. As a sort of personal virtue by which the company benefits, they channel ambition into the company rather than into themselves and try to establish higher and higher foundations so that the next generation to run it can succeed even more than they did.

When we look at the great enduring companies it seems that many have been passionate about something, such as a vision or founding ideal, just as the founders at the Infancy stage were passionate enough about something in order to start the business in the first place. Great companies are often focusing on something more than just profits such as a vision or ideal that generates profits and also attracts great employees (talent) who want their lives to be about something that is a larger mission. If your company is known for pursuing a higher mission, that in itself can attract the right type of people who would otherwise work elsewhere.

When a company broadcasts a clear ideology that everyone knows about, this positioning or branding tends to attract people to the company whose personal values are compatible with those same core values. Like-minded people tend to come to together because of a similar ideology, and so you will often find people attracted to working for a company which has a similar vision to their own. Professionals seeking jobs are typically looking to join a firm with an attractive world class vision where they can contribute as part of that bigger mission. Great companies might appear boring from the outside but they are often filled with people of intense professional will who are demanding of themselves and diligently devoted to a greater cause.

Warren Buffett tries to purchase controlling stakes in this type of company, namely a company that isn't a flamboyant highflyer and doesn't seem flashy but is devoted to its profitable and easy-to-understand business model. He has explained countless times that he looks to invest in businesses that will stand the test of time and reward investors over the long-term because they operate with a durable competitive advantage. He wants to invest in well-managed lasting businesses - companies with stable returns protected by a "moat" against competition. He wants businesses that can be run by idiots ("I try to buy stock in businesses that are so wonderful that an idiot can run them") to get brilliant results because they are based upon brilliant processes.

A moat, reminiscent of the water surrounding a medieval castle to protect the fortress from attack, is like a monopoly. It is the ability of a firm to protect its market share and profits from competing firms. To Warren Buffett, a moat is the ability of a company to keep competitors at bay for a long period of time so that it can continually rake in profits from its products and services. Buffett has said, "The most important thing is trying to find a business with a wide and long-lasting moat around it ... protecting a terrific economic castle with an honest lord in charge of the castle."

The Business Mission

The profitability of a company is important, but once again we must view those revenues as the byproduct of a service mission that provides value to society. Any company can find ways to make money by selling shoddy products, but the trick is to succeed gallantly with a higher contributive, service mission. The mission or purpose of the firm answers the question "Why?" In other words, why what it does matters and what difference it is making in the world. As the founders of Hewlett-Packard once said, bigger is only better if it is making a contribution to society. When companies instead focus consistently on what they can do better than others they can become highly profitable, but they can become great if they build their sense of purpose around core values and principles that give their work meaning.

What are some examples of a larger business mission, motivating purpose or fundamental reason for existence beyond just making money? Johnson & Johnson stated its business mission as alleviating pain and disease in the world. This is its constancy of purpose, which guides its operations and innovation. Boeing's mission is to pioneer aviation, which is why it continually works on introducing revolutionary planes. Walt Disney says its core purpose is to make people happy, which explains its many business projects. 3M is focused on innovation with a core purpose of solving problems innovatively. Walmart's purpose is "To give ordinary folks the chance to buy the same things as rich people." Hewlett-Packard has the core purpose of making technical contributions for the advancement and welfare of humanity. Starbucks was built on the idea of being "a third place" escape between work and home where people could purchase an affordable luxury after a stressful day. Merck's core purpose is to preserve and improve human life – to make quality products for a better life. George Merck, president of the company from 1925 to 1950 and chairman from 1949 to 1957, set the tone for these core values and standards when he gave a famous speech proclaiming "medicine is for the patient (rather than for profits)."

All businesses exist for the purpose of performance, and sometimes the business mission is more mundane such as offering reliable express service (Federal Express), or quickly delivering fresh hot pizza to your door (Domino's Pizza). The main thing of your business doesn't have to be earth-shatteringly inspiring. It doesn't have to change the world. It doesn't have to contribute to humanity in an outstanding social way, because it is there to perform a function, and all functions do not fit into the same category of greatness. Nevertheless, there should be a main thing about a business - an idea, vision, mission or "constancy of purpose" embodying the highest ethics, principles, values and vision - that isn't a worthless pious platitude. This constancy of purpose and highest vision should concretely guide its strategies, growth and decision-making processes.

For instance, Merck has participated in quite a few projects which never seemed directed toward profitability at first glance. Rather, they seemed to show an active interest in the welfare of humanity in accordance with its mission statement. In the 1940s Merck gave away its valuable patent rights to streptomycin, the antibiotic cure it found for tuberculosis, because too many lives were at stake. Tuberculosis was one of the deadliest diseases in history at the time, a "Great White Plague" that was killing one out of every seven people in the United States and Europe. Merck therefor donated the patent rights to Rutgers University so that the medicine could be licensed to multiple manufacturers for production. Even now Merck continues to develop and give away free river blindness medicine too. Just these two initiatives alone have been a great boon for humanity.

Why these decisions? George Merck once explained, "We try to remember that medicine is for the patient. We try never to forget that medicine is for the people. It is not for the profits. The profits follow, and if we have remembered that, they have never failed to appear. The better we have remembered it, the larger they have been." In other words, profitability is necessary, but only as a means to achieve a more important end.

These values and this type of core ideology serves as a source of guidance for Merck and is like a bonding glue that holds it together. Like a grand strategy, definite principles guide the company as it grows and expands. By *aligning* with these higher principles, which need no external justification, Merck has built something great, preeminent and lasting. The structure of the company has been built around this mission, and we can say that its success, as we have seen elsewhere, has been due to the principle of aligning with the standards that produce progress and prosperity.

In addition to a mission, there should also be a set of core values that establish the rules and boundaries that define a company's personality, and which provide a final "should/shouldn't" test for decisions and behaviors considered by the firm. Core values, as a guide to decision making, help to keep company executives and employees from becoming "errant men of business" who betray the people by trading humanity and integrity for profits. They abandon the status of humanity for financial gain. Confucius commented, "The gentleman is versed in what is moral. The small man is versed in what is profitable."

A perfect example of this can be seen in a crisis that happened to Johnson & Johnson when in 1982 seven people died after taking cyanide-laced extra-strength Tylenol sold in five Chicago stores. The Chairman of

Johnson & Johnson, James Burke, subsequently received the Presidential Medal of Freedom for what he did next. Under his leadership the company spent $100 million to recall 31 million bottles of Tylenol, patiently explained to the press everything that was happening, and then relaunched the product in tamper-proof packaging two months later. Because of his decision to do what was ethically right, despite the costs Burke saved the Tylenol brand and the reputation of the company.

The Johnson & Johnson credo had always stated that the company was responsible first to its customers, then to its employees, and next to the community and stockholders in that order. Since the credo gave first priority to the consumer, Burke said its core values made it clear what he had to do despite the cost – "the credo made it very clear at that point exactly what we were all about. It gave me the ammunition I needed to persuade shareholders and others to spend the $100 million on the recall. The credo helped sell it." A company expresses its personality through its values and these actions demonstrated the values of Johnson & Johnson and its chief executive. The behavior of a company should align with core values like this.

You don't need to have a celebrity leader, you don't need to be in a "great" industry, you don't have to pay the highest salaries, and your product ideas don't have to be the very best in order for your business to succeed and excel. However, what helps is to define your business as having a higher mission, which will help to guide it to greatness. For instance, Walt Disney makes great movies but its greatest creation is the company's ability to make money. Most firms can benefit by finding meaning in a higher mission and by establishing a set of enduring guiding principles it will never compromise upon for short-term expediency or financial gain. Without a set of core principles and higher mission, firms can easily end up like a bankrupt Enron.

Furthermore, you need to create a strategy for profits and growth using valuable principles pioneered by Jim Collins in *Built to Last* and *Good to Great* such as the Hedgehog Concept, Big Hairy Audacious Goals and Profit per X. For example, the "Profit per X" principle for managing companies to excellence is as follows: if you could pick one and only one ratio such as profit per x, cash flow per x, revenue per x, etc. that you would systemically work at increasing over time in order to improve the economics of a firm, what X would have the greatest sustainable impact on its economic engine?

For Gillette (which makes disposable razors and shaving supplies) the ratio is profit per customer, for Walgreens it is profit per customer visit, for Nucor (which manufacturers steel) it is profit per ton of finished steel, and for Wells Fargo it is profit per employee. Each firm creates a growth and profit strategy based around maximizing its own Profit per X figure. The denominator you choose represents your unique approach to scaling your business, and you should manage your firm by working on improving this ratio by taking it into consideration for strategy choices.

The process to becoming a great firm is essentially the following. You first discover the main economic driver(s) of your business, create a set of indicators that measure them, make sure everyone understands those measurements, align your goals, strategies, tactics and organizational design around them, link measures and activities with rewards and recognition, give people the training they need to execute the strategy to maximize them, create goals for everyone, and review performance on a daily basis. What you measure as a metric that encapsulates your economic engine must unify the company.

Collins, who is also author of the excellent book *Built to Last: Successful Habits of Visionary Companies*, felt that the best companies followed a single-minded objective (called the Hedgehog Concept) of trying to be the best in the world at something. They become deeply passionate about something after they understand what drives the company's economic engine and start incorporating that singular objective into management and marketing strategies. For instance, once Walgreen determined that it wanted to be the "most convenient drugstore with high profit per customer visit," it took this simple singular concept and implemented it with fanatical consistency as its company strategy. A single-minded, hedgehog-like focus on this strategy propelled it to greatness.

Collins wrote, "It embarked on a systematic program to replace all inconvenient locations with more convenient ones, preferably corner lots where customers could easily enter and exit from multiple directions. If a great corner location would open up just half a block away from a profitable Walgreens in a good location, the company would close the good store (even at a cost of $1 million to get out of the lease) to open a great new store on the corner. Walgreens pioneered drive-through pharmacies, found customers liked the idea, and built hundreds of them. In urban areas the company clustered its stores tightly together, on the precept that no one should have to walk more than a few blocks to reach a Walgreens. In downtown San Francisco, for example, Walgreens clustered nine stores within a one-mile radius. Nine stores! If you look closely, you will see Walgreens stores as densely packed in some cities as Starbucks coffee shops in Seattle.

"Walgreens then linked its convenience concept to a simple economic idea, profit per customer visit. Tight clustering (nine stores per mile!) leads to local economies of scale, which provides the cash for more clustering, which in turn draws in more customers. By adding high margin services, like one-hour photo developing, Walgreens increased its profits per customer visit. More convenience led to more customer visits, which, when multiplied times increased profit per customer visit, threw cash back into the system to build even more convenient stores. Store by store, block by block, city by city, region by region., Walgreens became more and more of a hedgehog with this incredibly simple idea.

"In a world overrun by management faddists, brilliant visionaries, ranting futurists, fearmongers, motivational gurus, and all the rest, it's refreshing to see a company succeed so brilliantly by taking one simple concept and just doing it with excellence and imagination. Becoming the best in the world at convenient drugstores, steadily increasing profit per customer visit – what could be more obvious and straightforward?"[19]

There are countless books available on what a company needs to do to thrive and become more profitable, and I'll summarize them by stating that a company needs a coherent strategy like this, but also needs to try a lot of other innovative stuff and keep what works. It should always be tinkering to improve its processes. Continuous improvement should become an institutionalized habit. It should benchmark to find out what works best at other firms, tinker to improve those processes, and constantly pursue innovation to satisfy customer desires otherwise competitors will catch up and overtake it, especially if it rationalizes that sunk costs should impede modernization efforts, new technologies and new innovations that might retire existing products or procedures. It must focus on creating underlying advantages over rivals. It must try to capture customer mindshare by owning words in the marketplace that matter, such as Volvo owning the word "safety" while Google owns the phrase "search engine."

A "good to great business" should focus on profitable niches that produce a disproportionate share of profits. It must advertise a strong brand promise to customers, as do cities and countries. It must be constantly focused on product improvement to meet changing customer needs, and the company must discard anything that is outmoded or obsolete. It has to test lots of things to see what works while accepting that mistakes will be made, but always maintain this valuable risk-taking attitude because this is how progress is achieved. Businesses must embrace a mindset of never-ending, continuous innovation because today's unique product or service becomes a commodity tomorrow, so innovation is the way to control your destiny because it is the engine of sustainable growth needed for survival. Therefore "Fail fast, fail cheap" is the right learning cycle to instill within businesses because they must innovate to stay alive, and innovation involves risk-taking and failures they must learn to digest. Businesses entail risks so companies must learn how to take them and manage them skillfully. Once a business finds a strategy that works it should

---

[19] Jim Collins, *Good to Great: Why Some Companies Make the Leap … and Others Don't*, (Harper Business, New York, 2001), pp. 92-93.

stick with it to grow its profits and sales.

Just as species must evolve to thrive, businesses must try lots of different approaches when facing challenges until they stumble upon something that works to solve their problems. Small opportunities, small risks and incremental gains can sometimes grow into unanticipated large strategic shifts, so never overlook the small but definite improvements you can make in business processes and functions. A business should constantly work at self-improvement, adopting the view "it's never good enough" since many companies reach a complacent phase where they don't just stop at getting better but start ignoring customers and then lose their business lead over others.

Also, never forget that many companies benefit from big, challenging, visionary projects/goals that can stimulate progress to move them forward in revolutionary ways. These are what Collins called "Big Hairy Audacious Goals." Talent loves to advance their learning, contribute their talents and be challenged, so you must give them some audacious goals! As Doug Hall says, they want to be involved in "Cool Sh*t That Matters." Companies thrive when they chase after big projects in line with company values that have a clear finish line which doesn't have to be explained, and which get employee juices flowing. Everyone benefits from a shot of inspiration and motivation, so companies need to give employees a chance to make a name for themselves and show what they can do by posing challenging projects. This type of challenging attracts the best talent to firms, who want to feel part of something exciting and greater than themselves that moves them forward. Most people in life are looking for a feeling of unity with a greater purpose.

And now, the typical story of impermanence, transformation and incessant change repeats itself. Eventually company leaders pass on, products become obsolete, new technologies emerge, markets change, customer tastes start to differ, and employees come and go. However, the core principles and ideology that guides and inspires a company should endure as the institution. Through thick and thin, through boom times and recessions, through cyclical uptrends and downtrends or economic highs and lows, a company must stick to its core values and ideology.

Satisfying customer desires and fulfilling their needs through your products and services is a way to create merit. Doing so in a way that uplifts the marketplace, raising everybody's standards, also produces merit because this is another type of contribution to society. A company should hammer out a core set of values for itself for providing a contribution to society through its product or services. It should align the company's goals, strategies, tactics and organizational design not just around profitability but around a core ideology of values and a higher purpose for being that serves some greater good. To truly become great, companies need to get rid of any misalignments they see within themselves and reward behaviors in line with their core values and goals.

We need a new paradigm across the world for corporations other than the purely competitive objective of maximizing profits and shareholder value. Companies must not only deliver financial performance but should be encouraged to make a positive contribution to society, benefitting not just their owners but their customers, employees and communities. In other words, instead of simply maximizing profits to benefit shareholders companies should also start to better benefit stakeholders, which is a result that will produce a better outcome for all.

A Schedule That Helps Alignment

In *Mastering the Rockefeller Habits*, Verne Harnish revealed an optimal company meeting schedule to help institutions seamlessly align their financial goals with the company's mission, values and ideology. In *Make it Big! 49 Rules for Building a Life of Extreme Success*, millionaire real estate developer Frank McKinney's explained how he did this in real time for himself.

In order to provide his business with a higher mission other than that of just making money, which he recognized is not a cause in itself of becoming happy, once a year McKinney would set aside some time to review the purpose of his business and try to see it from a higher perspective. Every year he would go through the exercise of hammering out a core ideology of purpose and values that embodied a higher service mission other than just profits, and then he sought some way to align his goals, strategy, tactics, actions and schedule around that higher mission. The method he used of maintaining alignment throughout the year demonstrates how to stay in touch with a higher purpose or calling even though there is the ever present requirement of profits.

McKinney wrote, "This simple planning process—setting aside one weekend a year to create a new personal vision statement, and then taking a couple of hours each Saturday to establish the goals that will help me turn that vision into reality—has been the bedrock underlying my success for the past 10 years. Once I started doing this, I found a marked change in my life and in my results. Sure, I was accomplishing more, since I was taking the time to plan my week. But more than that, I was linking my weekly goals to the vision of who I wanted to be. ...

"A personal vision and mission statement is the agreement you make with yourself that this is who you want to be, how you want to act, what you will and won't do, and how you want to appear in the world. It's also a living, breathing document that will change over the years. I know there are some people who like to create 5- and 10-year plans for their lives, but I'm not one of them. Sure, I can have a sense of who I want to be 10 years from now, but I have found that redoing my vision every year keeps it fresh. It allows me to take into account the progress I have or haven't made and set my direction based on what I see as my next step. After all, I have the big picture of my highest calling ... that pulls me toward my ultimate future much more strongly than a 5- or 10-year plan. ...

"Having a mission or vision statement for your business is the first step. Tying it to your goals is the next. Do your quarterly or yearly goals have anything to do with your mission? ...

"The last step is to make sure your daily efforts represent the goals you've set and the vision you've created. When your business spends its days pursuing goals based on your corporate vision, your customers as well as the business community will see you as having integrity. And isn't that the kind of reputation you want?"[20]

Grand strategy, asabiya, innovation trends that move progress upwards, economic cycles that go up and down, customer focused products, business purposes and missions ... all these concepts are related to values, virtue, and merit. They should help you realize that success, longevity, prosperity, progress, ascendancy, superiority, predominance or preeminence are all related to an alignment with higher goals and principles other than just the typical competitive pursuit to "maximize profit." They are achieved by targeting something higher that involves more humanistic ideals of values, virtue, service and merit.

---

[20] Frank McKinney, *Make It Big! 49 Secrets for Building a Life of Extreme Success,* (John Wiley & Sons, New York, 2002), pp. 31-32.

7
PRODUCTS

"Innovate and invent, but then uplift the market by using a unique selling proposition to broadcast your special benefits that explain why you are dramatically different. Align your entire marketing strategy with the USP."

Like civilizations, empires, countries, innovation cycles, boom times, and even companies … products don't last forever either. They all have a life cycle that begins with their birth and ends in their death. For instance, in my own lifetime I can remember each new innovation in the realm of audio recordings, and how each one became largely irrelevant when a new invention arose to replace it. The vinyl record, for instance, was replaced by reel-to-reel recordings. Reel-to-reel tape recordings were then followed by the cassette tape, the 8-track, CD compact disk, mp3 file, DVD and now Blu-ray disc.

Innovation changes the demand for everything. At one time people traveled by sandals, then by bicycle, next by train and automobile and now by airplane. Who knows what will come next? The longevity of a product is never assured.

Among other things, the longevity of countries, empires, cultures and civilizations is dependent upon the strength of their asabiya. Without unity, within these large groups of men and women you will eventually see fracturing and then destruction. Furthermore, the new generations that are born, or immigrants who do not adopt the national ethos, replace the oldest generations and mindset and progressively weaken the group asabiya if they do not cultivate the same virtues.

The longevity of empires and countries is also dependent upon their execution of a grand strategy for prosperity, just as is the case for companies that want to go from being good to great. The importance of cities bobs up and down dependent upon their economic success, which in turn depends upon how well they align with a number of prosperity principles too. Economies everywhere fluctuate due to cyclical forces, and companies become profitable powerhouses within this fray when they adopt highly motivating visions to guide their growth and set out to truly service customers.

From larger units down to smaller units, survival *and* prosperity are linked to the principle of adhering to virtuous purposes that build merit. To survive and thrive, groups of men must align themselves with prosperity forces and principles that embody virtue, values and merit.

Now we are down to the smallest unit of a company, which is a product or service. About 80-90% of all new products fail despite what are often viewed as brilliant innovations. In order to possibly cut down on this high failure rate we should ask ourselves what controllable set of principles account for a product's profitability and longevity. That's what we want to tap into or align with when designing new products and innovations.

Products that provide enough value or service to customers in an economical fashion tend to stay alive, and we can therefore say they "earn merit" by fulfilling customer needs or satisfying customer desires in this way. If you help someone achieve what they deeply wish or desire, as long as it is a virtuous satisfaction aren't you engaged in a meritorious activity? To create a winner you should ask yourself what type of benefit or value your product/service will provide to customers. What will it do for them … what's in it for the customer? If your new product or service cannot produce sufficient benefits, back to the drawing board you must go.

In other words, for a product to survive and become a "big hit" winner it has to offer benefits to customers. It has to provide value. It has to be of service. It has to in some way encapsulate a service merit of filling a need. It has to do all these things better than competitors, which means better reliability or cost effectiveness or some other cherished parameter of betterness. Once you determine what the meaningfully unique benefits and values are that it provides you must then broadcast them everywhere with advertising to obtain customers, otherwise the product (and possibly the company) will not survive without sales.

If a product/service is not sufficiently different from what the marketplace already offers then a company must go back to the drawing board and redesign it to make sure it is meaningfully unique. Its design or formulation should, in a manner of speaking, raise the marketplace by propelling competing offerings to a higher level of innovation or quality.

This capitalistic emphasis on improvement in order to garner sales is one of the ways in which we move civilization forward. By creating better products you create merit for society.

After you create a new product or service with sufficient benefits, the next question is how to effectively sell those products or services. What principles must your marketing and salesmanship efforts align with in order to effectively promote that product or service and bring in sales, which are the life blood of a business?

The answer to this question requires that you deeply understand the value proposition that your product/service represents to potential customers, and that value package needs to be condensed and presented in a succinct but attractive message called a "unique selling proposition."

Simply put, a unique selling proposition or USP is the value message promoted to the public about a product or service in order to get people to buy it. It encapsulates the meaningful value or benefit that customers will receive when they obtain it. People purchase a product or service because they believe it will satisfy their needs, wants, wishes or desires by delivering a satisfaction they imagine. Rendering positive benefits to others to satisfy their needs/desires is certainly a virtue or form of merit, and the USP tells you what those benefits are.

The unique selling proposition is the core principle for successfully marketing products and services. It is the foundational base of all good marketing. It is an overt, unique claim or promise of benefits about your business, product or service that you can broadcast to the public, and which distinctly differentiates your product/service from its competitors. It must be so strong, attractive and compelling that it motivates people to buy.

The famous business and management expert Peter Drucker once said that businesses have two functions - innovation and marketing - and the USP embodies both! It embodies marketing because it is the fundamental basis of all marketing done for a product, and it embodies innovation because the product must be meaningfully unique and different from all competitors. That newness or difference is what you advertise to the public.

When you are designing a new product it has to compete in the marketplace by offering benefits to customers, and something must make it unique enough to differentiate it from its competition otherwise it would just be a "Me too" challenger in a crowded marketplace that the public might easily ignore. When you are marketing a product/service you must announce to the world its greatest, sweetest benefits and what exactly makes it unique so as to differentiate it from its competitors. All of this is embodied in the USP.

Cities and countries cannot be guaranteed any sort of preeminence forever, but they can prolong their economic standings and maintain their populations by following certain principles. For instance, they can promote themselves in the most winning fashion to attract residents, talent, companies, trade and investment. They can also try to attract businesses of the most aspiring (rising) new economic sectors. These are just a few of the common principles for their success.

What can companies do for the goal of attraction? They can try to attract the right employees, and the right type of customers that need their product's attributes. The method that maximizes their profits and prolongs their survival along these roads is excellent marketing that promotes the product's USP.

The famous advertising man Rosser Reeves (*Reality in Advertising*) taught that a USP should possess three major characteristics:

- It should promise a *big benefit or buying advantage* for potential customers. It should boldly broadcast, "Buy this product and you will get this specific benefit." Its message should entail "benefit, benefit, benefit for you." It should answer the customer's question, "What's in it for me?"
- The unique selling proposition should be *dramatically different* from what competitors are claiming. In other words, it should dramatically differentiate the product from the competition. The value proposition should be so unique that other competitors cannot claim the same advantages. It should promise something that competitors do not offer and dramatically differentiate the product/service from everyone else.
- The proposition should be so strong, appealing, exciting, motivating or compelling that it can pull in new customers. In other words, the offer should be so appealing or compelling that *it causes people to act …* they encounter the USP, next investigate the product or service and then buy it. It should motivate action – it should cause people to buy.

Doug Hall, author of *Jump Start Your Brain*, stated that the USP contains three musts:

- It must always identify an *overt benefit* of your of your business, product or service and advertise it. It must reveal what is in it for the customer if they engage with you – a meaningful benefit promise. Customers are always thinking, "Why should I care?" so it must tell potential purchasers what they are getting for any money they spend.
- It must always communicate what is *dramatically different* about the business, product or service being advertised from all competitors. This is whatever it is about what's being sold that makes it meaningfully unique versus what the competition does. The message

is about meaningful uniqueness – the product/service needs to offer a meaningful point of difference. It must be really different on a way that matters.

- It must possess natural credibility for its claims by providing *a real reason to believe* them which is a type of product or service proof for what makes the product's promise possible. The "reason to believe" might be a product guarantee, warranty, quality measurements, the company's reputation, or even the product's pedigree. The USP must provide natural proof for the meaningful benefit claims so that they are believable so it explains how the offering will deliver on its promises.

Thus, a unique selling proposition must telegraph the promise of big benefits to potential customers; claim the product/service is unique and dramatically different from competitors; provide a seal of credibility and believability that is self-evident; and must be so persuasive, compelling and motivating that it prompts customers to act (buy the product or service). It must telegraph a simple, focused value proposition to potential customers that outshines the competition. Most of all, it must encapsulate the meaningfully unique benefits and values that the product/service produces.

There are several additional characteristics to a USP that make it work. It should grab attention by being interesting or exciting; being focused it doesn't try to appeal to everyone; it is short, simple, concise, memorable and easy to communicate; it is economically feasible enough to support a business; and its design is such that many business functions can support it with a congruency of alignment.

In *How to Create a Million Dollar Unique Selling Proposition* I detailed ten ways – the largest collection you can find in print – to come up with a unique selling proposition for a product, service, company or even person. A USP can help with city marketing or national tourism efforts as well.

The USP should become the foundational core of anyone's marketing efforts as well as the focus of any attempts at product creation. If you want to fix a company's marketing you must first start with its products and their USPs. If a new product idea doesn't have a good USP then go back to the drawing board and create a better product. The new product doesn't offer a big enough benefit or isn't dramatically different from everyone else? Then go back and redesign it, which is the gist of innovation. Your product or service should add value to the world by being an improvement or meaningful difference. If you are not meaningfully unique then you better be cheap to survive.

Marketing and innovation efforts should always be conducted with an attractive, saleable USP in mind. Marketing and sales efforts should align with the promises of the USP too.

CULTURE, COUNTRY, CITY, COMPANY, PERSON, PURPOSE, PASSION, WORLD

10 Ways to Create a USP

The first way you might go about creating a USP is to write down all the reasons a customer might buy your product/service, cross out everything on the list that is also true of the competition, and then from this final list of unique benefits turn the biggest one into the USP.

The second way to create a USP is to create a list of all the features, properties, attributes, performances, applications and characteristics of a product or service, turn those features into benefits, and then keep looking at all the benefits until the most important, unique, and believable benefit jumps out that you can advertise widely as the USP.

The third method is to pose a question to the company's customers similar to the following: "What is the biggest frustration/worry/thing you hate most about dealing with [the product, industry, business, service]?" Once you have an answer indicating some type of performance gap in the market, next you must recreate the product or service to fill it. Redesigning a product or service to fill that need is innovation, and afterwards you can then broadcast its unique attributes and how it fulfills a need as the USP.

The fourth method is to record a salesman or yourself explaining to people how a product or service is different from others and fulfills the market's needs in a way that competitors do not. You record yourself while pretending you are talking to a customer or friend, or do so in real life, and start conversing using the following format, filling in where appropriate: "You know how most [state the pain or problem of your industry using an example the prospect is familiar with]? Well what I do is [state the solution by listing what your product or service does]." This then becomes the basis of the unique selling proposition.

The fifth method is to articulate a product's or company's *real reason for being* – its purpose for existence – and turn that into a USP. You must articulate the original reasons the product, service or business was created in the first place. What gap in the market was it trying to fill? Obviously someone saw a need or opportunity, so why did it come into being? What were the founders or creators trying to improve upon or accomplish? What mission was it created to fulfill? Why would someone even bother to get into a highly competitive business unless they could offer certain unique benefits to customers that no one else could provide? Turn those reasons into the USP.

In the sixth method, based on Doug Hall's work with product creation, you must identify the overt benefit of the product/service, why it is dramatically different from others, and the reasons potential customers should believe this. This becomes the basis of your USP.

97

The seventh method, based on the work of Dan Kennedy, is to answer the following question posed by a customer: "Why should I choose your business/product/service versus any and every other competitive option available to me?" Similarly, "Why should I do business with you above any and all the other options available, including doing nothing at all or continuing with whatever I am doing now?" When you determine the unique buying advantage they receive from the product/service then you have the basis of a USP.

The eighth method for discovering a USP is simply to ask customers why they buy from you and what's most important to them about buying your type of product or service (and how they know they have it). Then you need to promote the reason they buy *your* product/service. To get more customers of the type you want, do more of the same thing those customers desire, or do something even better. When doing this type of customer polling, you must make sure to ask customers how the product or service can be improved and then do that. Never forget the principle of improvement, which is innovation. This is what renders benefits to others, and is the merit you want to be creating with your business and life.

The ninth method is to use any of the previous methods for deriving a unique selling proposition, and then write out a first draft of a USP. Next, study two or three competitors and write out their USP. Now that you have yours and theirs, rewrite your USP to make yours more distinctive and different from what others are saying/offering.

The tenth method is that of preemptive marketing, which is to be the first one in your business or industry to promote a particular benefit of your product/service that everyone similarly provides, but to claim it as your own simply because no one else bothers to promote it. In this way you can "be first" rather than "better," and everyone else who tries to promote themselves as offering the same benefits afterwards is seen as a "Me too" copycat. This can become the basis of your unique selling proposition.

Once a company has created a profitable USP for their product/service that brings in customers and sales, it should align its internal functions, company structure, R&D efforts, marketing efforts and even appearance with that unique selling proposition. It should stamp every brochure, newsletter, email etc. that comes into contact with customers with the USP – which it has already determined is *the biggest and most attractive benefit it can promise to potential customers*. The USP is the message that brings in sales and revenue. A company should therefore promote this message everywhere because it is the key to getting new business. A firm that aligns itself with a profitable USP is giving itself the greatest chances for success and prosperity. This is what brings in sales and customers – revenue for surviving and thriving.

Creating a high performance USP and marketing it everywhere is actually a noble thing for two reasons. First, because by publicizing a USP you will help attract customers who need your benefits, thus making it possible to serve them and answer their needs. Second, because it advertises uniqueness and benefits it will elevate the marketplace by raising the quality of offerings available to the public. Competitors *will have to improve their own products and services to compete* when they see that someone else is grabbing market share. A good USP forces products to evolve into something better, thus benefitting mankind.

Therefore, a company should promote its carefully formulated USPs every chance it gets. A unique selling proposition is a success plan for business profits similar to a destination branding and placemaking plan for a city or grand strategy for national prosperity. A company should organize business operations around it so that it can deliver upon the USP with more effective excellence. Once a company finds one that really works then its office design and décor, how it answers the phone, how it replies to customer complaints and so on should all reflect the message of the USP.

Personal Branding

You can even create a USP for people in order to help them promote their professional standing or career. A personal USP can help you get a job, get a raise, or get customers for your business. The purpose of creating a personal USP would be to help you present an image of yourself to the world that you want presented – for very particular reasons - rather than have the world create a reputation for you that you don't want. By creating a personal USP you define the way by which you want to world to think of you.

When you create a unique value proposition for a person, which encapsulates how they are to be known, this is like creating a personal brand for the individual. For instance, when we think of the actor Cary Grant an entire set of images involving charm, sophistication, style and grace come to mind. They embody the image of a happy, amusing fellow at heart who has masculine glamour - a Western civilized man made perfect. This is his acting persona. Cary Grant embodies what seems like a happier time, an amalgam of the traditional and modern, the elite and commons, the high and low, the great and good. This is his personal branding, the persona he created. Grant said of his acting persona, "I pretended to be somebody I wanted to be until I became that person, or he became me." When you needed this set of attributes in a movie actor then you called for Cary Grant.

You can create a brand image for yourself like this also by cultivating yourself in a certain way, as explained in *Color Me Confucius* and *Buddha Yoga*, until you actually become a certain way. President Eisenhower, for instance, became known for a sunny disposition despite a personal problem with anger issues, and accomplished this feat by cultivating his outer demeanor. George Marshall also cultivated himself to develop certain personality traits that he became known for, including honesty and directness, as did George Washington.

Personal branding is basically the task of positioning yourself so that you become known for special descriptive features you want in order to gain some personal benefit. For instance, when working for a company you might want to build up a particular image or reputation for a special type of excellent performance in order to help advance your career. A professional who owns their own shingle (such as a lawyer, accountant, doctor, etcetera) might want to cultivate a certain brand image to help sell his or her services.

A brand image, or personal USP, can help you achieve greater success in life by positioning your reputation in a way you deem fit. Since it is putting out everywhere that you perform or exist in a certain (desirable) way, if you create one you must always try to live up to it. As with placemaking, you cannot present empty slogans to the world and expect people to believe them.

By publicizing your own personal brand, those who come in contact with it will be taught to think of you in a certain way and associate you with something you choose to stand for. It will shape people's opinions about you by design so you must construct it carefully based on your desired positioning. If you have a personal brand or USP, it will train people to think of you as different from others in a certain special way. Think of it not just as a USP for selling you but as a public reputation.

A personal USP can create an identity by which you are known that will usually hold for a long time, unless you change it or fail to hold up to the portrait it promotes. Thus, it can be used to help create an image and any specific type of success or reputation you want. When you want to create a personal brand for yourself, the goal is to become positioned as "the" immediate name that people think of when they cogitate about what you want to represent. A personal USP or brand is used to help you win "top of the mind awareness."

Personal branding can help you firmly establish a professional reputation of having the exact, specific characteristics you want to be known for by the public. Thus it can help promote whatever you want to be known for concerning your personality, service, career or business and you can use this to create prosperity. It's about creating the message of a public persona that is disseminated everywhere, telling people what you publicly represent. In a professional life you want to *create that image intentionally* by what you say and do (and market) rather than have a lesser reputation crafted by others or by default. You want to purposely sculpt out the public image you want of yourself. You want to be the one who decides the way by which you will be known.

How do you come up with a personal USP to help change your fortune? You must identify a number of characteristics you want others to recognize about you, figure out the most important ones, and then put those together in an attractive, memorable way to establish a personal branding statement. The rule to follow is:

Your Skills/Specialization + Your Authentic Personality/Passion + Your Distinctive Differentiation + Persistent Visibility + Market Relevance/Needs = Your Branding Statement

Once you have your personal USP, you should reduce that branding identity to a few short sentences called an "elevator speech" or "pitch statement" that you can use to introduce yourself. This is a 15-30 second verbal business card, a scripted introduction you can use when you meet someone new and want them to know what you represent or do. It is like an executive summary of your personal USP positioning designed to make a positive impression and arouse potential interest in you.

For instance, famous marketer Dan Kennedy's USP/elevator speech runs as follows: "I devise direct marketing strategies for all types and sizes of business that eliminate all the fat and waste from their advertising and increase the productivity of their sales people by at least 1000%, Guaranteed." A children's book author once said, "I give kids awesome dreams – I write books for children so they can fall asleep at night." A meditation instructor once said, "I teach people how to attain daily peace of mind and contentment in a world of constant stress so that they can deal with life more easily and find relaxation wherever they go."

This quick, clear and compelling statement – exactly the characteristics you want in a simple but powerful self-promotion – is a perfect branding statement, elevator speech and personal USP. To formulate a powerful message like this you must determine how you wish to be known, and by asking that question this might also help you think about your life's mission or higher calling!

If you want to promote your career or professional experience then you must figure out what you want to be known for, always work towards solidifying that image by perfecting your actions and behavior in those directions, and then formulate this into an elevator speech that you can commonly use to position yourself when connecting with others so that people will adopt those same ideas to describe you by default. People don't like to think too hard, so you win in positioning by essentially telling them how to describe you to others.

What excellence, specialty or expertise do you want to be known for? You need to make it easier for people to remember you by formulating the perfect message they might use to do so. This is just one of the many ways to force yourself to live up to higher standards in life and through this alignment also get ahead.

8
PEOPLE

"Over the ages men have painstakingly built civilization and culture by aligning themselves with higher principles of ethics and virtue. In this way men have far separated themselves from being just animals. When it comes time to make an important decision involving self-interest and the profits of money, power, fame and status that all desire but which are fleeting, consider the troubles of that ages long struggle."

Why do some people prosper in life while others do not? It isn't just due to luck. You will find a large proportion of people who became successful and prosperous because they adhered to tested principles such as saving, minimizing debt, working hard, investing, and so forth. By aligning with such principles you will give yourself better chances to move ahead in life.

Prosperity principles don't just include the ones found within *Think and Grow Rich (Napoleon Hill)*, *Super Investing (Bill Bodri)*, *Rich Dad Poor Dad (Robert Kiyosaki)*, *The Science of Getting Rich (Wallace Wattles)*, *The Millionaire Mind (Thomas Stanley)*, *Secrets of the Millionaire Mind (T. Harv Eker)*, *Automatic Wealth (Michael Masterson)*, or *The Success System That Never Fails (W. Clement Stone)*. There are also said to be karmic principles of giving that bring the prosperity of health, wealth, happiness and peace of mind in return.

Errant Men of Business

Some people in life may seem to enjoy prosperity, wealth and high position as a result of evil actions they commit such as drug lords, crooked politicians or just ordinary errant men of business, which is what you will encounter most often. What are "errant men of business"? They are people who compromise professionalism, ethics and their bond with humanity because of a pursuit of profits. They may outwardly look like elegant gentlemen and act like outstanding members of society, but errant men of business have put aside a bit of their humanity and responsibility to fellow humans and/or the environment we live in because of the pursuit of money. Men choose their values in life, and errant men of business choose the wrong ones. Here are some blatant examples of errant men of business who were willing to commit gigantic crimes that harmed other human beings just for the sake of income.

When the top executives of America's cigarette companies ignored all the evidence and maintained that there was absolutely no relationship between smoking and cancer, and also attempted to engineer cigarettes to become more addictive while standing in front of Congress testifying that cigarettes were not addictive, they proved themselves to be errant men of business. They choose profits over lives.

When Nestle distributed the company's baby formula to nursing mothers in the Third World for free, it gave just enough baby formula so that while using it the lactating mothers would stop producing their own milk. Poor Third World mothers and their babies then became entirely dependent on the free formula, but they could not afford to purchase it after the trial period ended and a mother's milk had dried up. Thus, thousands of babies died. Through this marketing method used in order to increase sales, Nestle executives became errant men of business. To their own credit, however, they vowed never to let such behavior happen again.

When vaccine manufacturers consistently deny that vaccines cause damage when the evidence strongly indicates otherwise, and when the medical community persecutes doctors and parents who say this damage exists or that the number of vaccines children must receive is far too high, these resisters to truth all become errant men of business who have chosen profits over the welfare of human lives.

When Monsanto sued farmers because its own GMO products contaminated their fields, its executives and lawyers became errant men of business who tried to reverse roles and turn their victims into criminals. The company in hundreds of publicized actions has shown that its executives have consistently positioned it incorrectly in the moral universe. Monsanto has many times demonstrated a principle that when profits become the only destination that matters then people will often choose the low road to get there, and will try to hide their actions because they know they are wrong. How can you say you didn't know your actions were wrong if you take steps to hide them because you know they will provoke criticism?

When investment banking employees mislead their clients to sell them lousy products to clean out their own books, and then bet against those same products they just sold to "suckers," they become errant men of business. When the executives of Goldman Sachs perjured themselves before Congress about the doings of their firm (claiming that they were not significantly net-short the mortgage market when their own position was internally called "the big short" that accounted for 54% of the company's risk) they became text book models of errant men of business.

The top salesmen at many firms regularly lie to their clients/customers through exaggeration and omission in order to make sales. They too have become errant men of business. Too many people have lost their moral center in this way solely for the pursuit of profits.

Many other examples can be given of lawyers, lobbyists, government officials and politicians who abandoned their ethical training in the pursuit of profits and self-interest. To sacrifice morality for money is to enter the folds of the errant men of business.

Capitalism is by far the best economic system in the world, but there should be limits on what companies are allowed to do within capitalism in order to make profits. Many corporations, if given the blessing of legality, would readily suck every drop of blood out of human beings and kill a large swath of humanity. For the United States, one of the kisses of death that accelerated this reign of terror appeared when it gave corporations the same rights as individuals and allowed them to contribute to political campaigns, thus sealing the fate of its citizenry to be treated as unchecked plunder. The U.S. did not design its system towards just ends. It forgot that people are primary, not corporations or other non-living entities, and there should be principles to follow that are higher than making money. The lives and rights of people are to be protected, not profits and money-making.

We must all treasure human life more than profits, doing the right thing in all situations even though money tempts us to do otherwise. This is a humanistic principle ignored by modern profit-seeking corporations. After all, they are supposed to maximize profits, and humanistic values often stand in the way of that objective. The principle of the Confucian, Buddhist Hindu and Christian ways, on the other hand, are to live an ethical, moral life that contributes to communities rather than preys on society by making money through immoral means.

"Success" or "station" in life are typically measured by the level of wealth, power, position or prestige we achieve. However, Confucius reframed the importance of these results by recasting true success in life in terms of a man's behavior. He focused man's efforts on becoming what has been translated as virtuous individuals, nobles, gentlemen of benevolence, exemplary men and women, or men and women of consummate conduct.

Confucius taught that whether or not you become an exemplary man or woman of consummate conduct is determined by whether you are living according to the highest ethical values and trying to become more that way because of a devotion to self-improvement. This effort, rather than a high birth, is what makes someone truly noble. You are noble because of what you do and what you are working on becoming as a person, not because of the family you were born into.

An example that comes to mind is Dwight Eisenhower, who wanted to be a leader, and knew he needed to project optimism and confidence to do so. Therefore he especially worked on developing a moderate, balanced and cheerful demeanor. After recognizing that anger was his major personality flaw, Eisenhower did a number of things to tame it such as writing down the names of people he hated on slips of paper, tearing them up and then throwing them away. In time he developed a mature temperament by attacking his faults through self-cultivation, which is one of the signs of a man of consummate conduct.

You don't have to be perfect to pursue "consummate conduct," but you must be working on decreasing your faults to become better. Since it takes an average of six days to acquire a new habit, you just have to keep working at yourself to see improvements in any personal behaviors you want to change. Men and women of consummate conduct – upstanding people who radiate goodness and virtue – were not born that way but *made themselves that way*. They worked at becoming better people. They cultivated themselves through efforts of self-improvement.

Men of Consummate Conduct

The opposite of errant men of business are therefore the men and women of self-cultivation who work at developing consummate conduct. Like others they work on their own businesses or work as employees for someone else, but they also work on improving their knowledge, skills, habit energies, and behavior. With the capital and skills they accumulate in life they try to improve/help others and improve/help the world. Instead of just taking from the world they try to turn around and make a contribution so that the world becomes better off because they were here.

As exemplary models who followed this pattern we can turn to great men such as Benjamin Franklin, Andrew Carnegie, Sylvanus Thayer, James Jerome Hill, Julius Rosenwald, Johns Hopkins and David Packard. All of these men were known for having high values and they engaged in self-cultivation (self-improvement) efforts and consummate conduct. They all lived honorable lives, even in business, and made efforts to give back to others and help society using whatever funds they had accumulated in life.

To understand this ideal of the businessman who was a contributor to society and who also followed the pathway of merit-making and consummate conduct, it is best to start out with Benjamin Franklin, one of the most important Founding Fathers of America. Franklin was clearly both a man of self-cultivation as well as a servant of mankind who helped to greatly develop American civic society and culture.

Franklin served in a number of professional positions during his life – printer, postman, soldier, ambassador, inventor. When he was starting out in the printing business he worked on cultivating his character so that he was known to the locals as someone ambitious, hardworking and trustworthy. As he once wrote, "Industry, perseverance, and frugality make fortune yield." From wise dealings he accumulated enough wealth and steady income that he could retire at age 42, which was primarily due to property investments and his printing business. He became one of the wealthiest men in Philadelphia.

Not just a printer himself, Franklin multiplied his income by setting up printing joint ventures with other individuals where he would buy the printing presses and typeface for the partnerships and thereafter receive a share of the business profits. In his autobiography, Franklin explained the reasons why his partnerships normally succeeded while those of others often failed. "Partnerships often finish in quarrels; but I was happy in this, that mine were all carried on and ended amicably, owing, I think, a good deal to the precaution of having very explicitly settled, in our articles, everything to be done by or expected from each partner, so that there was nothing to dispute, which precaution I would therefore recommend to all who enter into partnerships; for, whatever esteem partners may have for, and confidence in each other at the time of the contract, little jealousies and disgusts may arise, with ideas of inequality in the care and burden of the business, etc., which are attended often with breach of friendship and of the connection, perhaps with lawsuits and other disagreeable consequences."

Franklin was also a scientist who investigated the characteristics of electricity, and the first person to chart the Gulf Stream. He also was the inventor of various items such as bifocals, an odometer, and the Franklin stove. Thinking of the public, Franklin never patented his inventions to make money from them but made them freely available to the public, commenting that he "should be glad of an opportunity to serve others by any invention of ours; and this we should do freely and generously."

Benjamin Franklin's many contributions to the United States changed the landscape of its political, educational and social life. In particular, he greatly benefitted the city of Philadelphia. It is said that he was behind nearly every project that made the city of Philadelphia a more attractive place to live. In Philadelphia he founded the first lending library, the first scholarly voluntary association focused on mutual improvement (the Junto), the first fire department and postal system.

One of Franklin's talents lay in bringing together people for benevolent purposes, which is what he did to also create the Philadelphia Hospital, and the Pennsylvania Academy that is now the University of Pennsylvania. In all these projects Franklin rarely presented himself as their proposer and avoided taking credit. Rather, he adopted the lifelong habit of presenting philanthropic ideas as a "scheme of a number of friends." He also pioneered the mechanism of the matching grant while raising funds for the Pennsylvania Hospital, proposing that the colonial government contribute the same amount to its establishment as private contributions. He did so many good things for the public that we can only remember his words, "It is prodigious the quantity of good that may be done by one man, if he will make a business of it."

Toward the end of his life, Franklin wanted to give even more back to both Boston and Philadelphia, the city of his birth and his city of residence. He therefore funded two small gifts in his will totaling 1,000 pounds sterling (around $4,500) that were to be placed in a trust and invested for 100 years. Upon the 100-year mark, 75% of the accumulated sum was to be used to help tradesmen and fund civic projects, but the rest was to be invested for another 100 years, after which it was to be given in full to the cities. Thus he blessed future posterity in this way as well.

Thanks to the miracle of compound interest, after 100 years the trusts in Boston and Philadelphia were worth $400,000 and $100,000 respectively, prior to disbursements. One hundred years later they had grown to $4.5 million and $2 million due to interest compounding, a great gift to the cities. Thus, two hundred years after he lived students who were studying to become tradesmen have been able to go to school thanks to the money Franklin had set aside years ago. As you can see demonstrated by this case, in his dealings Franklin often developed projects that he thought might extend great benefits to posterity.

Despite his many accomplishments, perhaps Franklin's greatest legacy was his emphasis on the cultivation of virtue found in his autobiography. He created a famous ledgering system for self-improvement purposes that helped him reduce his vices and cultivate positive character traits, and its story has been a great contribution to American culture. The details of the method (and its usage by famous individuals) can be found in *Color Me Confucius*.

It was Franklin's own cultivation emphasis on self-improvement that transformed his personality into that of someone who was quite affable and could get along with others. For instance, rather than outright contradict individuals and create arguments, Franklin adopted the habit of first saying, "It appears to me …" or "If I am not mistaken …" His affability enabled many of his legislative proposals to be accepted by his fellow countrymen and allowed him to become one of the most well-liked of America's Founding Fathers. Franklin showed how a person's life and character could become a noble one through constant self-assessment.

Another man known for outstanding character traits that he had cultivated was Sylvanus Thayer, a military officer who was ordered by President James Monroe in 1817 to become the superintendent of West Point in order to bring order out of the academy's laxity and chaos. Under his stewardship West Point became America's first college of engineering and the world's finest military academy. The West Point motto of "Duty, Honor, Country" originated with Thayer.

Often compared to a kind of military monk, Thayer established West Point's ideals and values system – high academic standards, strict discipline, the demerit system, summer encampment, and an emphasis on honor and responsibility. He also ran West Point as a meritocracy when it came to admission standards, which was a revolutionary idea at the time since it avoided any sort of favoritism. Thayer would discharge cadets he believed were unsuited to West Point's ideals, and finally left the institution only when President Jackson, for political reasons, would by presidential order return a cadet that Thayer had dismissed.

Thayer then went to Dartmouth in order to establish a civilian school to train engineers. He even donated $40,000 to the trustees of Dartmouth College "for the purpose of establishing ... a School or Department of Architecture and Civil Engineering," which thus created the Thayer School of Engineering. On the front of Cummings Hall at Dartmouth is carved a quote from Thayer on the purpose of the school: "To prepare the most capable and faithful for the most responsible positions and the most difficult service." Thayer was a true man of consummate conduct who executed his duties according to the highest principles, which he tried to instill within an educational system that would train men.

Andrew Carnegie, born in Scotland, was another self-taught man of virtue who devoted his accumulated wealth to helping the world. He created the largest iron and steel maker in the world, and became one of the richest men in America. As a youth he lacked a formal education, just like Benjamin Franklin, but like Franklin also became an avid reader to teach himself. He was proud of the fact that he succeeded in many of his ventures because he always surrounded himself with men having more talents than himself. He was also known for his honesty, once returning $500 he found while a messenger boy. Imagine the temptation to keep such a sum of money that was equal to ten times his wages!

While most of his fellow capitalists financed their various business projects with watered down stock, Carnegie chose a higher road by founding all his early organizations as either partnerships or associations, and invited partners into the business based on the character and quality of the men. Therefore he was one to share his wealth and success with others. Many of the heads of his departments became millionaires due to their relationship with Carnegie.

In his autobiography, which revealed his own style of self-cultivation, Carnegie wrote that men should invest in themselves and become master of topics of their own choosing. They should seek knowledge and wisdom and value contribution in life rather than just money. Success, he felt, came from being open with others and treating people well. People desiring success should enlarge their circle of friends, be eager to repay favors and share their success with others. Most of all they should learn to control their mood for he felt that a sunny disposition was worth more than a fortune.

Carnegie thought you should divide a man's life into a period of accumulation and then distribution of the wealth you had accumulated during life. In the second half of one's life he felt that a person should divest themselves of their overabundance, saying that it was a disgrace for a man to die rich. Specifically, he said "The man who dies rich dies disgraced." Within ten years of his death he had given away 90% of his fortune, and at one time write, "Try to make the world in some way better than you found it is to have a noble motive in life."

Altogether Carnegie used his great wealth to establish 2,811 public libraries around the world and donate 7,689 organs to churches. He established Carnegie Technical Schools, which is now Carnegie Mellon University. He also established the first modern philanthropic organization, which is the Carnegie Foundation. In the purposes for the foundation, Carnegie thought that a man should give away most of his wealth in philanthropy to help others, but should spend it in the right way so as not to encourage idleness or destroy men's ambitions.

Although a businessman most of his life, he thought deeply on how to use his wealth to help society and put his thoughts into an article, "The Gospel of Wealth," which has become one of the most important American blueprints for philanthropy and benevolence. In the *The Gospel of Wealth* he articulated his view that the rich were trustees of the wealth they had accumulated and urged wealthy individuals to use their funds to help their communities and to promote the welfare and happiness of others.

Realizing that money given to others often leads to bad results, he felt that charitable funds should be used to support libraries, hospitals, universities, meeting halls, recreational facilities and other projects that would strengthen individuals so that they could become more independent and productive. He said, "Neither the individual nor the race is improved by almsgiving. The best means of benefiting the community is to place within its reach the ladders upon which the aspiring can rise." He wanted to give people the means by which they could help themselves.

This is why Carnegie funded institutions that would help men improve themselves, such as libraries. Carnegie had two major reasons for supporting libraries: (1) the books would enable people to educate themselves and, (2) as an immigrant himself Carnegie believed that America's newcomers needed to acquire cultural knowledge of the country that a library would make possible. Because of his support for various self-improvement measures like this, Carnegie was one of the most influential philanthropists in American history whose deeds greatly improved America's society and culture.

Another philanthropist who greatly changed America is someone few know about. Most people have heard of the company Sears Roebuck founded by Richard Sears, but they usually haven't heard of his partner, Julius Rosenwald. Rosenwald took care of operational measures at Sears Roebuck, which sold mail order catalog products during an era known for deception and slick sales pitches. He was the one who set the high standards of company honesty so that customers who ordered by mail got exactly what was described in the company's mail order catalog. Because of Rosenwald, Sears Roebuck offered one of the first money-back guarantees in America and pioneered the trusting "send no money" advertisement.

In addition to his fame for instilling Sears's high ethics, Rosenwald became known for his multi-million dollar philanthropies. He also encouraged other wealthy individuals to support good causes on their own, feeling that "property entails duties." Although Jewish, his philanthropy transcended all barriers of religion, race, and nationality. As an example, he advanced the cause of black education by funding Booker T. Washington's Tuskegee Institute and by building thousands of schools (4,977 to be exact) for black children in the rural American South. He also built several dozen YMCAs across America and one of Chicago's largest philanthropic housing developments.

Rosenwald was one of America's most innovative donors. When building schools, for instance, similar to Franklin he insisted that his donations would not be made unless matched by the local residents, and usually maneuvered local and state education authorities into participating. He did not give anonymously because he felt that the credibility from his name, when visibly supporting a project, was valuable to the project, but he also fought to keep his name from being affixed to any properties or institutions. This is why he is largely unknown, which is thanks to his good motives of keeping his name off projects.

Rather than establish a charitable fund to exist forever like the Carnegie Foundation, Rosenwald established a philanthropic fund to "sunset" itself out of existence in order to achieve better immediate results. His fund was instructed to use all of its monies for charitable purposes within 25 years of his death. Rosenwald had seen how other foundations had lost their way by eventually focusing on their own perpetuity rather than their mission of getting things done. Therefore he felt that foundations should attack national problems with urgency and use up their funds within a reasonable time while leaving future challenges to future philanthropists.

I actually agree with this approach rather than the perpetual (and bureaucracy-laden) philanthropic foundation that sometimes gets co-opted by intelligence agencies for their own purposes. Personally I would like to see more philanthropy flowing from individuals alive than being directed by the wills of dead rich people. Help to society usually has a greater impact today than if it is delayed. When you give, what a joy it is to see most of the action is made during your lifetime when you can still correct matters such as preventing other entities, who want to take control of your wealth, from usurping your original intent. If you want to give and make a difference you should start giving now, and put a sunset limit on unexpended philanthropy after your death – perhaps thirty years or half of a Kondratieff cycle. When people say, "I'm going to leave it in my will" rather than donate to good causes now, what they are really saying is, "If I could live forever I wouldn't give any of it away."

Rosenwald gave to many projects but once said, "I can testify that it is nearly always easier to make $1,000,000 honestly than to dispose of it wisely." Andrew Carnegie also said that it is more difficult to give money away intelligently than to earn it in the first place. Before you give you must think about the consequences of your gift, such as unintended side effects, and whether an organization can actually manage the project you sponsor.

The founder of *Forbes* magazine, B.C. Forbes, once described Rosenwald by saying, "The most notable thing about Julius Rosenwald is not any superhuman business ability, nor any phenomenal smartness in seeing and seizing mercantile opportunities. ... The greatest thing about Julius Rosenwald is not his business but himself, not what he has but what he is, his character, his character, his personality, his sincerity, his honesty, his democracy, his thoughtfulness, his charity of heart, his catholicity of sympathy, his consuming desire to help the less fortunate of his fellow creatures." Rosenwald was therefore a man who not only cultivated himself and consummate conduct, but held to a mission to help others.

Another man of interest was James J. Hill, a Canadian-American railroad executive who had the dream of building a transcontinental railroad line across the United States. This was purely a business aspiration, which is perfectly fine. It is what Hill did along the railroad line to help promote his own interests that was special, which is to help build towns, settlements and businesses that would help make the railroad a success.

Hill's railroad, the Great Northern, purchased land along the railroad from the federal government and resold it to settlers at cheap prices. He also sold lumber across his rail lines to encourage the construction of towns. He invested in founding schools and churches for these new communities and developed livestock and crops that settlers could profitably raise near the railroad. Furthermore, he often offered free breeding stock to farmers to help them build the livestock business in the region. He taught farmers better farming methods and erected large grain elevators in Buffalo. Basically, the Great Northern invested in people and communities in order to build its own business (just as Henry Ford had raised his workers' wages so that they could buy his automobiles) and there is nothing wrong in that! He enriched the local economies in order to sell more product and become richer himself. Rather than just take, he raised people up in order to raise up his own fortunes.

Hill also maintained a strong philanthropic presence all his life, such as founding a theological seminary at St. Paul. The interesting thing about his life is that he used his business interests to perform a great social service in building up the Pacific Northwest region (Montana, Minnesota, Oregon and the Dakotas), thus playing a critical role in developing the U.S. through his railroad empire. His work caused the founding of countless cities and hundreds of thousands of farms, which helped bring great prosperity to the masses.

Johns Hopkins is yet another American entrepreneur who amassed a great fortune through a career in banking, real estate and investing and who thereafter determined to devote the gains he had acquired to the public. He became Baltimore's guardian protector and greatest philanthropist by endowing it with a university, hospital, medical school, school of nursing, and orphan asylum for black children. During the Civil War, he rushed to offer Baltimore emergency aid by loaning the city half a million dollars. As Carnegie had suggested, after making provisions for his family Hopkins devoted most of his fortune to the service of humanity.

Nine months before he died, Hopkins wrote an instructional letter to his hospital's trustees informing them of his charitable objectives: "The indigent sick of this city and its environs, without regard to sex, age, or color, who may require surgical or medical treatment, and who can be received into the hospital without peril to the other inmates, and the poor of this city and state, of all races, who are stricken down by any casualty, shall be received into the hospital, without charge ... You will also provide for the reception of a limited number of patients who are able to make compensation for the room and attention they may require ... you will thus be enabled to afford to strangers, and to those of our own people who have no friends or relatives to care for them in sickness, and who not objects of charity, the advantage of careful and skillful treatment." These ideas are similar to those of the Aravind eye hospital system that we will later encounter.

David Packard, the co-founder of the electronics giant Hewlett-Packard, is another industrialist businessman who made his mark through ethical business practices and because of giving back to society through philanthropy. Hewlett-Packard became one of the most admired electronics companies in America with Hewlett spearheading product innovation and Packard focusing on managing the company. The corporate environment it created was incredibly unique, and was the forerunner of Silicon Valley. So well known were Packard's administrative skills with technology issues that during the Nixon administration he was asked to take a hiatus from HP during the middle of his career and go to Washington to serve the country as Deputy Secretary of Defense.

The two Hewlett-Packard partners developed a special set of business principles, known as the "HP" Way, which reflected a corporate morality that included high respect and concern for employees. They promised never to layoff employees and offered a generous profit-sharing plan. During economic recessions, for instance, to avoid layoffs the company scaled back on working hours instead. Part of the HP way was to also avoid long-term debt, which could become crippling during an economic downturn, and not to enter into any businesses that the company did not understand.

Packard donated more than $1 billion in charity during his lifetime, and his projects included founding the Monterey Bay Aquarium and helping Stanford University through generous contributions. The university stated upon his death, "Dave Packard, along with his wife, Lucile, and his partner, Bill Hewlett, have shaped and nurtured this university in ways that can only be compared to the founders, Jane and Leland Stanford." Like many other businessman who became wealthy only because of the free enterprise capitalistic system that existed, Packard also funded political institutions that promoted free enterprise such as the Hoover Institute and American Enterprise Institute.

The Ethics Test

All these men lead honorable business lives, and also were devoted to the people. They showed that you can and should pursue business profits, but it should be done in the right way so that you do not become an errant man of business. Remember the few fundamental rules of ethics that should apply even in business: do not do to others what you do not want them to do to you, do not aggress in any way upon a person or their property, and before you undertake any questionable action you should consider whether its righteousness could be justified as universal law.

The profit motive can warp even the best of minds so that a man becomes unclear and unsure what is proper. Therefore all sorts of tests for business ethics have been proposed for judging the righteousness of behavior such as the conscience test (does this go against my conscience?), the consequences test (would this behavior create bad consequences?), the broadcasting test (what if everyone knew I did this?), the religion test (does this go against the rules of my religion?), the fairness test (is this fair to all the parties involved?), the "what if everybody did this?" test and all sorts of other tests to judge the properness of actions.

It is not just the propriety of business decisions that makes you a man or woman of consummate conduct, but what you do with the wealth you accumulate from business, meaning money derived from *others*, that also matters in life. Wealth can be used entirely for personal consumption, or it can be used in other ways, some of which might benefit mankind. Which will you choose?

John Wesley spoke towards this saying, "Do all the good you can, in all the ways you can, in every place you can, at all the times you can, with all the zeal you can, to all the people you can, as long as ever you can." Buddhism espouses, "Do everything good you can, eliminate any evil when you encounter it, never block any unborn good from arising, and never let any unborn evil ever arise." Jesus said to do unto others as you would have them do unto you. Master Zeng explained of his teacher Confucius's way, "The Master's Way lies in exerting all of one's effort and relating to the needs of others. That is all." These are just some thoughts to think about. I personally ask people to act wisely and think about doing whatever would elevate you the most above your animal nature.

Excel at Your Career

All these wealthy individuals pursued business or occupational interests, but they particularly distinguished themselves by adhering to strong ethical principles and values in their lives. This doesn't mean that they never made mistakes or offended others, but that they indeed tried to do their best and avoid obvious wrongs. Some were also known for continual efforts at self-improvement. For instance, Franklin and Carnegie both taught themselves by reading books, Thayer and Franklin were famous for the work they did on cultivating their personal behavior, all of these men were famous for working hard, and Carnegie and Rosenwald were especially known for the virtue of honesty.

The second commonality to these men of consummate conduct is that they all made efforts to contribute to society with a determination that something could be done to make things better. They all contributed a share of their efforts to the greater good and tried to leave the world a better place than when they found it. This usually meant some form of philanthropy, but the important point is how they went about it. Some concentrated on helping their city, some on helping their country, some on helping individuals, and others (such as Carnegie) worked on spreading a positive influence throughout the world.

All these men had different philanthropic priorities, different views on what would make society better off, and thought deeply about the effects of charity on human nature. For instance, Carnegie believed that charity could be injurious unless it helped the recipients to become independent of it. Therefore he searched for ways to help society without creating dependence. As the multi-millionaire John Rockefeller said, who was also known for his own large charitable activities, "The best philanthropy is constantly in search of the finalities - a search for a cause, an attempt to cure evils at their source." Rockefeller focused on curing the source of society's ills rather than battle the never ending symptoms of illnesses. He attempted to give to charities that would address the root of problems rather than their outcomes.

Rockefeller was by no means a man of consummate conduct in his business affairs. Nevertheless his views on philanthropy are instructive to would-be benefactors since he also thought deeply on the issue due to the fact that he was one of the largest philanthropists in the world. He was allegedly influenced along these lines by a meeting with Swami Vivekananda in 1893, who urged him to use more of his philanthropy in projects to help poor and distressed people. Rockefeller later wanted his family to share in a sense of duty to improve the common good, and felt that family traditions played a critical role in the transmission of these values from generation to generation.

You don't have to be a multi-millionaire superstar like some of these individuals to become a man of consummate conduct. There are only three requirements to becoming noble: devote yourself to the road of self-cultivation (self-improvement), keep to your ethics and the road of high principles during difficult times, and try to be of service to others. Those are the three principles: cultivate yourself to improve yourself; never depart from your values in life including for the needs of your occupation or money-making; and practice compassion in trying to give back to others.

The third principle is to help society with your resources (time, money, talents, etc.), however great or scanty they might be, to be of service when and wherever you can. In other words, try to contribute however you can even if it is but small. Some people have such few resources that there is little they can do but survive, and thus cultivating your own character and behavior, even in the midst of poverty, is still the core essence, rather than giving, of what makes one the most noble.

There are only three main options for how to make a living in the world. The major alternatives are that you either (a) work for the government, (b) work for yourself in your own business or profession, or (c) work for someone else such as a boss, company or institution.

If you work for yourself then it might be possible to make your occupation part of your life purpose or life mission, but this is rarely the case. Sometimes a business or career just puts food on the table without any higher mission, and that's perfectly fine because that *is* the major purpose of a business or career. Who can criticize the fact that businesses need profits to survive and we all need money to live? The problem is that many service sector jobs, which are the only paycheck opportunity available for some individuals, provide no useful skill sets and leave people with no productive abilities whatsoever. Life seems empty if it is just about work, and for people who only have such jobs they must seek a higher purpose.

People can easily become stuck in meaningless office or retail jobs and squander away their lives knowing that they are accomplishing nothing meaningful other than earning a paycheck. This is why I say you have to build skills, opportunities and activities outside of work, for in this case this is the only place to find a higher meaning or purpose for your life. It is also why I tell people to use their free time and freewill efforts, however small, to train to become Bodhisattva protectors or build merit in this direction. Those who become Bodhisattvas are the ones who already did this.

Most people wish that their work could serve a larger purpose in the world and constitute a higher mission, but you cannot guarantee that this will be possible even when you *do* own your own business. Therefore it is a matter of what you do *outside of work* that will or will not create a more meaningful life. We make a living by what we get from others, but we make a life by what we give. This is what you need to consider.

Few people are lucky enough to be able to build their personal career on a compelling mission that gives meaning to their work. Just because you want to organize your work and life around a mission doesn't mean that you can make it happen. If transforming missions that supported a life were that easy to create then everyone would be doing them, but you rarely see this happening. Most of us have to work for others to make a living.

When you do work for someone else you should always do your best and work your hardest to excel for your boss. Be loyal, think of your boss's interests, and try to give him and your company your best. A man or woman of consummate conduct sets the goal of contributing wherever they can and being the best they can be at whatever they do. You should approach your work like a true performer who takes this to heart, which is the proper career principle of alignment.

Advertising legend David Ogilvy once advised the following in a 1977 interview with John Chrichton, "Be more ambitious. Don't bunt. Try to hit the ball out of the park every time. Compete with the immortals. Try to make whatever you do the greatest that anyone has ever done. You won't always succeed but reach for the stars. Don't bunt. Be more ambitious. Ambition is the key. Try to do remarkable things. Try to be great. It is the lack of ambition that cripples most people." Ogilvy's principle of success was that you should always try to excel. He promoted the ideal of not only doing your best, but "to be always pre-eminent," which is the Greek idea of *arête*. The Greeks stressed this ideal of "excellence" not just by an emphasis on cultivating an ideal physical form. They stressed that individuals should us all their faculties to full force for effectiveness in the world, which is *arête*. In the Greek view, one could only live up to their full potential by cultivating/involving all the abilities and potentialities available to humans.

If you work for the government as the third career option you will have a whole set of other behavioral expectations in front of you that are quite different from the expectations of the business world. However, you can still become a man of consummate conduct even though the establishment may think you are otherwise. A bit of advice that most often comes to mind for such a career originates from Colonel John Boyd of the United States Air Force. Boyd was a remarkable unsung hero in military history who revolutionized American military practice and policy by writing the first manual on jet aerial combat, spearheading the design of the F-15 and F-16, teaching the U.S. Marine Corps how to fight on the ground, and shaping the tactics which won the Gulf War. When he was hiring someone to work for him in the Air Force he would tell him the following, which has come to be known as the "To Be or To Do" speech:

"You are at a point in your life where you have to make a choice about what kind of person you are going to be. There are two career paths in front of you, and you have to choose which path you will follow. One path leads to promotions, titles, and positions of distinctions. To achieve success down that path, you have to conduct yourself a certain way. You must go along with the system and show that you are a better team player than your competitors. The other path leads to doing things that are truly significant for the Air Force, but the rewards will quite often be a kick in the stomach because you have to cross swords with the party line on occasion. You can't go down both paths, you have to choose. So, do you want to be a man of distinction or do you want to do things that really influence the shape of the Air Force? To be or to do, that is the question."[21]

Naturally this type of advice doesn't apply to all types of government jobs, but does provide some food for thought for government career professionals. As government employees often relate, if you step out of line to shake up the system you might lose your job or even get prosecuted, so every workplace by doing what is right has its own survival and flourish

---

[21] Robert Coram, *Boyd: The Fighter Pilot Who Changed the Art of War*, (Little, Brown and Company, Boston, 2002), pp. 284-285, 340.

rules that must be taken into consideration.

Most people are taught to follow their passion in life in order to develop a rewarding career. This and a lot of related advice can be traced back to mythologist Joseph Campbell's dictum to "follow your bliss." This sounds wonderful if you have a passion that people are willing to pay for, but most people don't, nor do they usually have skills in those areas that would produce an income. Who would pay to watch you play golf or tennis? The truth is that you shouldn't follow your passion but should bring it with you wherever you find yourself.

For instance, I might have an incredible passion to play basketball, but people certainly won't pay anything to watch me play because I don't have exceptional skills at either of them - I'm not good enough. I might want to grow roses, but there might not be enough money in it even if I become an expert at rose gardens. As Warren Buffett also said, his own incredible investing skills were only valuable because he was born in the United States, a perfect *location* where he had a chance to use them. Had he been born in Communist China his skills would have gone to waste. John Paul Getty also said he became rich (for awhile the richest man in the world, in fact) only because he was born at the *right time*, so the circumstances of *time and place* factor into whether you can become rich or not. It isn't just a matter of hard work, skills and interest. All sorts of other considerations and circumstances come into play as well.

In actuality, most people were not born with preexisting passions. However, we are all free to develop as many skills as we like and uplift our mental perspective to find a higher meaning in whatever we are doing. You can certainly cultivate more passion by changing this attitude and mindset. To live larger in life, you must adopt the viewpoint that your energies are being devoted to some higher purpose, such as in the story of the bricklayer who believed he was building a cathedral while his companions only saw themselves as building a wall. You must believe that your efforts are enriching the world in some way. You also don't have to be the singular hero of a social movement that wants to change the world either, but can simply be part of a larger cooperative effort shared with others. This is how most people at NASA feel about their work ... they feel they are part of a larger team that works on a joint mission. In identifying with the mission of a larger group, people can forget their private interests and lose themselves in the pursuit of larger communal ends.

This principle of looking for a higher meaning in what you do is championed in *So Good They Can't Ignore You* where Cal Newport masterfully points out that "following your bliss" fails to describe how most people end up with compelling careers. People are often taught to follow their passion but a passion mindset focuses on *what the world can offer you* (the value your job gives to you) whereas a more realistic craftsman mindset focuses on *what you can offer the world*. What can you offer that is of value to others? What can you contribute?

You can certainly make money at what the world will pay you to do, but don't expect the world to simply give you an exciting, valuable career because you want one. Having one is a rare luxury. Most people would love a job that allows them to be creative, make an impact on the world, and have control over how they spend their time but such jobs are rare and valuable, and the only way to get something valuable is to offer something valuable in return. For instance, a craftsman develops skills over time by devoting them to some calling. People will pay for the craftsman's work; he gets paid because he offers something valuable in return.

Most people usually want their work to serve a higher purpose but no one can guarantee that you will ever enter a profession of such caliber. You usually only get such plum jobs after you have already established that you have developed exceptional skills, like a craftsman. Compelling missions that give meaning to your work and provide you with money are the exception rather than the rule in life. Therefore it is often what you do *outside of work* that is where you will find a higher set of purposes in life.

Regardless as to how you feel about your job, the craftsman mindset is a reliable foundation upon which you can build a compelling career. It requires you to master the art of continual improvement at your job, which is the process of self-cultivation or self-perfection illustrated by the life of Benjamin Franklin, George Washington, George Marshall or even Andrew Carnegie who constantly looked for improvements that would cut the price of steel by even a few cents. A craftsman mindset requires you to relentlessly focus on the value you are offering the world. It asks of you to shine so bright that people won't ignore you.

You should think of it in this way. A *job* is simply a way to pay the bills. This is what most people have in life, so for most people meaning in life has to be found outside of their working job. A *career*, because you continually master new skills, is a path that leads to increasingly better work but a career may or may not provide much in terms of a higher purpose or mission. A *calling*, on the other hand, involves work that is an important part of your life and part of your identity so it might involve a life purpose or higher meaning. In all of these options you must avoid becoming an errant man of business, but focus on the possibilities of self-perfection, improvement and service to others.

Each of these alternatives has limitations or constraints on what it can provide you in terms of monetary rewards, feelings of satisfaction, and feelings of a higher purpose or mission. The hard truth is that you will usually have to find a higher purpose, mission or meaning in life outside of your job and career. It will usually be what you do outside of your working life that counts. That is where most people can contribute the most.

That being said, your work is going to fill a large portion of your life and while it might not amount to a calling the only way to become satisfied is to do great work. In any endeavor you find yourself you should try to do your best, master the skills of achievement, and try to contribute to others in a meaningful way.

Thinking About Life Purpose

How do you contribute to others? Aside from the service or value you supply through your work, Buddhists say there are three ways you can contribute to others, known as the three methods of offering. Normally these are thought of as three forms of charitable giving, but they are also three forms of cooperative contribution.

First, you might give wealth or resources to help others as a type of contribution. Second, you might provide others with some degree of fearlessness (confidence or protection) when they become anxious or afraid. You might give them hope or take away some of their concerns. Third, you might provide other people with teachings that can help their lives mentally, spiritually and physically, which is called giving Dharma.

These three ways of helping other people are called the three forms of offering or three ways of generating merit. Regardless of whether or not your business, job or occupation is fulfilling you can always practice some degree of the three forms of offering as a way of lightening the burdens of others, contributing to society and accumulating merit. As Aesop said, "No act of kindness, however small, is wasted."

We are all here in this world as stewards only, and take nothing with us upon our death. As living beings we have the power to do something for the lasting betterment of mankind that can help reduce the number of unhappy people around us, but will you take any such steps to help others? There is a domino chain effect from doing kind deeds such that kindness gets passed forward to spread everywhere, so whatever we do for the world can in one sense be viewed as immortal. Therefore why not take some steps to do something for others?

That being said, what star is your North star? What does your life truly revolve around? What do you really care about? Where do you want to make a contribution? What light do you want to see in the world?

Every now and then you must separate yourself from the script you are presently following in life and ask, "Is my life on track? Am I headed in the right direction? Am I satisfied with the plot that has already played out or do I need to change directions? What do I want my life to really be about and are my actions taking me there? Where *are* they taking me? Am I pursuing what others expect of me or my own dreams and aspirations? Am I being in my own identity or acting according to somebody else's expectations? What do I ultimately want to accomplish? Are my present goals even worthy of my time and efforts? Am I doing what I feel I am placed here on earth to do?"

By asking these questions you will determine whether or not you should be altering course and the direction in which you should be headed.

What else might you ask to spur the right sort of self-reflection? You should consider whether you are holding to your ethics and values in whatever you are doing, or sliding down the slippery slope that eventually produces errant men of business.

Try asking yourself, "Am I personally living my ideal of an honorable and virtuous life? Am I living with integrity? Is my present behavior reflecting my values? Would I be okay with my family and friends knowing what I do and how I behave? Am I cultivating my humanity?

Furthermore, "What do I ultimately stand for? Am I remaining silent, or am I standing up and raising my voice? Am I supporting the light that I want others to see? Am I following my inner voice?

"What am I trying to realize as my best self, and am I accomplishing that? Are my goals serving a higher purpose? Am I allowing myself to express my true self? Am I letting myself be happy?"

How about personal skills? If you are reading this you are obviously alive and intelligent, so you still have time to develop nearly any skill you want through self-study and self-effort. Years ago Earl Nightingale helped instill within America a characteristic of self-improvement and recognition of the need for lifelong learning by urging people to spend one hour per day studying a topic until they achieved basic mastery. The books of Daniel Coyle on developing talent, since it is something you develop rather than are born with, would also be immensely helpful in this area.

Along these lines you need to ask yourself, "What do I want to learn and master in life with the time remaining? If I have an aim of achievement then what must I learn for those accomplishments? How must I better myself and how do I better myself? How do I want to be in whatever I must do? Am I committed to my own individual excellence?"

What about the question of contributing to mankind? For this every small effort counts but you should always be asking yourself, "What is the ultimate purpose of my business, career or job other than just making money? Am I creating benefit for others and doing something that society finds useful? Am I helping to make a better future? At the end of my life, facing death, will I be able to say I did something and that it is better that I was here? Am I making the difference I want?"

This very moment you should pause and ask yourself what you can offer the world, and reevaluate what goals and activities seem worthy of your money, time, energy and efforts. With the time you have left, you should consider what type of positive impact you want to make in the world. A decomposing skeleton is what you will one day become, so with that finality in mind you should consider doing something starting *now*. Mother Teresa aptly said, "If you can't feed a hundred people then feed just one." Desmond Tutu said, "Do your little bit of good where you are; it's those little bits of good put together that overwhelm the world."

And finally, many life coaches ask people to consider the following legacy questions that are also useful to ponder, such as, "How would you like your obituary to read? What do you want to be remembered for after death … what is it that you want people to be reading on your tomb stone? What do you want to accomplish with the time you have left?"

I personally like to bring up the story of Linds Redding, a New Zealand-based art director who had worked at BBDO and Saatchi & Saatchi. Redding wrote an essay "A Short Lesson in Perspective" after he was diagnosed with terminal lung cancer, and being reflective before his death therefore penned the following:

> Perhaps I am not alone in this assessment. Many people have their own idea of a person's life, without knowing what really goes on, on the inside. Some even envy the lives of their friends and colleagues, without realizing, their lives are much better. Now that I am out of that life, I am able to have a different perspective of my old life.
>
> And here's the thing.
>
> It turns out I didn't actually like my old life nearly as much as I thought I did. I know this now because I occasionally catch up with my old colleagues and work-mates. They fall over each other to enthusiastically show me the latest project they're working on. Ask my opinion. Proudly show off their technical prowess (which is not inconsiderable.) I find myself glazing over but politely listen as they brag about who's had the least sleep and the most takeaway food. "I haven't seen my wife since January, I can't feel my legs any more and I think I have scurvy but another three weeks and we'll be done. It's got to be done by then. The client's going on holiday. What do I think?"
>
> What do I think?
>
> I think you're all fucking mad. Deranged. So disengaged from reality it's not even funny. It's a fucking TV ad. Nobody gives a shit.
>
> This has come as quite a shock I can tell you. I think, I've come to the conclusion that the whole thing was a bit of a con. A scam. An elaborate hoax. …
>
> Countless late nights and weekends, holidays, birthdays, school

recitals and anniversary dinners were willingly sacrificed at the altar of some intangible but infinitely worthy higher cause. It would all be worth it in the long run …

This was the con. Convincing myself that there was nowhere I'd rather be was just a coping mechanism. I can see that now. It wasn't really important. Or of any consequence at all really. How could it be. We were just shifting product. Our product, and the clients. Just meeting the quota. Feeding the beast as I called it on my more cynical days.

So was it worth it?

Well of course not. It turns out it was just advertising. There was no higher calling. No ultimate prize. Just a lot of faded, yellowing newsprint, and old video cassettes in an obsolete format I can't even play any more even if I was interested. Oh yes, and a lot of framed certificates and little gold statuettes. A shit-load of empty Prozac boxes, wine bottles, a lot of grey hair and a tumor of indeterminate dimensions.

It sounds like I'm feeling sorry for myself again. I'm not. It was fun for quite a lot of the time. I was pretty good at it. I met a lot of funny, talented and clever people, got to become an overnight expert in everything from shower-heads to sheep-dip, got to scratch my creative itch on a daily basis, and earned enough money to raise the family which I love, and even see them occasionally.

But what I didn't do, with the benefit of perspective, is anything of any lasting importance. … Economically I probably helped shift some merchandise. Enhanced a few companies bottom lines. Helped make one or two wealthy men a bit wealthier than they already were.

As a life, it all seemed like such a good idea at the time. …

Pity.[22]

What did a life lived 100% for work accomplish except work? Such individuals become errant men of living, squandering their life essence. If such a life is so great, why do people on their deathbed commonly look back and lament, "I worked too much and should have spent more time with my friends and family. I wish I would have let myself enjoy more. I wish I had travelled more."

Do you want to know what the definition of "folly" is? It is consuming the greater part of your life making a living rather than following an inner

---

[22] Linds Redding, "A Short Lesson in Perspective," Accessed July 19, 2018, http://www.lindsredding.com/2012/03/11/a-overdue-lesson-in-perspective/.

calling, great or small, that elevates and ennobles you and your life's activities. I remember listening to John Taylor Gatto recount Adam Smith's opinion that if you spend all your time and focus all your life on making money then it's a mark of insanity. All it buys you is a bad life. Nonetheless we should be grateful to those who do so because they assemble capital, pay the biggest price and create improvements for everyone else, but do you want to become like that yourself? Remember, this opinion/warning came from Adam Smith!

Are you living a life that is soul numbing in the pursuit of work, or are you actually doing something of consequential importance? Are you incorporating some downtime and fun or is it just seriousness all day long? Are you following your own dreams and aspirations, and ultimately carving out a life purpose or set of purposes in life that are meaningful to you or the world? Don't be a fence sitter anymore. Try to have the courage to take a few steps in the direction of your heart even if those things might be scary because they are unfamiliar. Get into some action - feel the fear and do it anyway.

These are issues that you should think about to help you decide what is truly meaningful to you in life. By pondering such questions you can slowly arrive at a mission, purpose or purposes within life that will make your life more satisfying.

As I point out in *Quick, Fast, Done* it is of great benefit to step back on a daily, weekly, quarterly and even yearly basis and consider some of these questions in order to help yourself stay on track towards achieving your personal goals of success and happiness. No one ever tells you to do this, but this is how you can make sure you continue to align yourself with the highest principles that bring both happiness and prosperity.

Most people are searching for a higher purpose in life and are craving to feel a sense of belonging to something with *gravitas* that is much bigger than themselves. They want to dedicate themselves to something greater than themselves, or at least identify with a larger entity or mission and feel part of it. They don't necessarily want a mission but are looking to be associated with a larger identity of excellence, grandeur, beauty or hope that is absolutely sublime and of which they can say, "I am part of this, I belong to this, I want to be connected with this." Throughout life people commonly strive for unity with Heaven, grandeur or some other type of greatness.

Thus people end up searching out their ancestral roots, absorb themselves with religion, promote customary traditions, or strongly identify with nationalism, team sports or some idealistic movement. It's all about looking for a larger identity of greater significance than their own small life. They are looking for a larger meaning by seeking something to align with other than to just trudge through the protoplasmic need to sustain the process of survival. One of the ways to feel you are greater is by seeking a sense of unity with a larger whole that represents a sacred mission of *gravitas*.

You cannot ask "why" about life or existence, but must find meaning in it by your own thoughts and actions. To live is the goal of life, so there is no meaning to it other than just living. Therefore you have to *create meaning in your life by your own thoughts and efforts*. You have to get in sync with the real you to find a personal meaning to life, a reason and purpose to live other than just survival that gets you up in the morning.

A life purpose is different than the purpose of life. It is you who must personally decide what to live for. Your everyday decisions are what bring meaning to the elements of your life, raising you upwards with nobility or not. The purpose or purposes of your life will be whatever you decide upon and work towards.

My suggestion is simple. Seek within to find your highest and best aspirations, and then align yourself with a set of values and ideals that represent those elevating aspirations on what you would like to do or become.

9
PASSION & PURPOSE

"Let no one be discouraged by the belief that there is nothing one person can do against the enormous array of the world's ills ... Each of us can work to change a small portion of events. And in the total of all those acts will be written the history of a generation."
- Robert Kennedy

We have already analyzed the fate of great groups of people that decrease in size from massively large cultures and civilizations down to progressively smaller entities such as countries, cities and even companies. Each of these entities has its own unique identity, sense of purpose, values, cods of behavior and strategy for survival. If each of these entities aligns with the principles of success then it survives and thrives, and the positive results of aligning with these values is sometimes called "an accumulation of virtue and merit."

Now that we have reached the smallest unit of size for social groups, which is the individual who has the choice to live an honorable life or not, and practice consummate conduct or not, we will proceed on an ascending arc to analyze the fate of increasingly larger groups of people united by common positive purposes, common virtuous values and a cooperative asabiya. However, this all starts with individuals finding their own purpose, mission or passion in life that they can use as their Pole Star for orientation.

Sometimes a person's life purpose turns into a great contribution for mankind although in most cases it does not. Most of us can only contribute a very little to those around us, and not much to others. All that matters is that people try to find themselves and some mission or responsibility in order to eventually pursue something that will give meaning to their lives, which is usually (but not always) a form of service. Meaning can come as a result of taking care of one's family, or it might come from a multitude of purposes that could include fostering a business or making some type of contribution to others. Even when business becomes the main purpose/concern of our lives, we all need to devote a little bit of time, effort or even money outside of our work requirements and the materialistic struggle for existence in order to help accomplish something wonderful for humanity.

Some people do find their purpose in life within their occupation, and some are lucky enough to find a passion that eventually becomes a career or larger purpose. Some people find their passion and purpose in following an interesting hobby or other pursuit that you or I might deem trivial. It does not matter whether your life purpose is something others appreciate or not because for most of us it is a personal, private matter. What matters is that you seek out a life purpose or purposes in life, to give your life a higher meaning. You want it to count. There are countless types of life purpose, but when you can align with a compassionate, giving purpose that renders helpful service to others you will generate an incredible amount of merit for freeing people from burdens of sorrow.

All people need a vision, purpose, passion, or mission in life that gives it some meaning other than purely the pursuit of survival. We have all heard the stories of individuals whose primary purpose was just working at their jobs, and after retiring they quickly passed away because they didn't have anything to do anymore. Since devotion to work was their primary purpose for living and they didn't cultivate interests outside of it, now that their job was over there seemed no more reason to live.

The great folly of most individuals is consuming the greater portion of their life running after money rather than fulfilling the mission of living purposefully. That mission does not have to appear within your job or career, and it does not have to be gargantuan either. However, it should be an ideal that keeps pulling you forward like a steady magnet. You simply must spend some time in pursuing other higher objectives outside of the basic materialistic needs for survival. This is the pathway of nobility.

If you say that money is the most important thing then you might spend your life completely wasting your time doing things you don't like to do in order to stay miserable doing things you don't like to do, and then might teach your children to follow the same erroneous pattern. When you don't find your purpose in life you will experience an absence of inner peace and a chronic, lingering dissatisfaction because you know that what you are doing is out of sync with your inner calling.

The poet Rumi once wrote,

There is one thing in this world that you must never forget to do. If you forget everything else and not this, there's nothing to worry about; but if you remember everything else and forget this, then you will have done nothing in your life.

It's as if a king has sent you to some country to do a task, and you perform a hundred other services, but not the one he sent you to do. So human beings come to this world to do particular work. That work is the purpose, and each is specific to the person. If you don't do it, it's as though a priceless Indian sword were used to slice rotten meat. It's a golden bowl being used to cook turnips, when one filing from the bowl could buy a hundred suitable pots. It's a knife of the finest tempering nailed into a wall to hang things on.

You say, "But look, I'm using the dagger. It's not lying idle." Do you hear how ludicrous that sounds? For a penny, an iron nail could be bought to serve the purpose. You say, "But I spend my energies on lofty enterprises. I study jurisprudence and philosophy and logic and astronomy and medicine and all the rest." But consider why you do those things. They are all branches of yourself.

Remember the deep root of your being, the presence of your lord. Give your life to the one who already owns your breath and your moments. If you don't, you will be exactly like the man who takes a precious dagger and hammers it into his kitchen wall for a peg to hold his dipper gourd. You'll be wasting valuable keenness and foolishly ignoring your dignity and your purpose.[23]

In studying the world's "Blue Zone" areas where many people live to be over one hundred years old, the longevity researcher Dan Buettner found that long lives were not tied to work but to having purposes outside of work, an *ikigai* or reason for being that was a source of value in a person's life. *Ikigai* means the reason for which you wake up in the morning, the things that you live for, the things that make one's life worthwhile. It includes strong connections with one's family and social connectedness - active connections or responsibilities within one's community and greater society. Without social connections and bonds that build a sense of belonging people tend to die much more quickly. The structure of everyday life that involves social bonds, social responsibilities and high connectivity tends to result in greater longevity. This holds true for individuals as well as

---

[23] Robert Ullman and Judyth Reichenberg-Ullman, *Mystics, Masters, Saints, and Sages: Stories of Enlightenment*, (Conari Press, York Beach: ME, 2001), p. 28.

for the fate of countries since a strong social fabric means a strong asabiya.

As stated, sometimes your purpose in life can be your career, but most times it is a passion outside of your work. Sometimes it is an activity that thrills you, interests you, excites you, or provides you with some sort of contentment. Sometimes it is a passion that can generate an effect larger than anyone could possibly imagine. None of these possibilities must be earth-shaking in their importance or reach, but let me recall several notable examples that might inspire you.

Here are just a few sample individuals who followed their personal interests and turned them into a career, calling or life purpose that had a great impact on others.

Billy Beane found his passion in studying baseball through statistics and invented the entirely new field of sabermetrics to predict player values and baseball outcomes. As a result of his passion, despite a great deal of initial opposition sabermetrics has made its way into a number of sports worldwide and totally changed the way that professional players are selected and teams are managed. It has become so prevalent that there was even a baseball movie made about sabermetrics - *Moneyball* starring Brad Pitt.

Bruce Lee found his passion in pursuing martial arts, and turned it into a martial arts movie career. He widely spread the message of martial arts and elevated the Hong Kong martial arts film to a new level of worldwide popularity and acclaim.

Nutritionist Adelle Davis had such a passion for natural foods that she wrote four books that ended up changing the American diet. Nutritionist Gary Null, with similar health messages to deliver, also made it his life's mission to spread the word about the ability of natural foods and vitamin-mineral supplements to heal.

Julia Child found her passion in French cooking, which she parlayed into career that brought French cuisine to the American public and changed the American dining table.

Lawrence Anthony found his passion and calling late in life by becoming a conservationist. Together with his wife, Francoise Malby-Anthony, the couple adopted the conviction that they could do anything if they really wanted it enough and so they started the South African game reserve Thula Thula in Zululand, South Africa. Anthony worked hard to rescue troubled elephants who would normally be shot due to their wild behavior. So effective was he that upon his death some of the elephants he worked to save came to his family's home to mourn in the way they normally do upon the death of one of their own.

The famous mathematician Leonard Euler found his passion in pursuing mathematics, producing 60 to 80 volumes of groundbreaking mathematics whose quantity has never been surpassed by anyone in the field. Similarly, Srinivasa Ramanujan, immortalized in the movie *The Man Who Knew Infinity*, found his passion and life purpose in the pursuit of mathematical number theory even though most of us would consider it useless.

Shakespeare, Bach, Rembrandt and Van Gogh all devoted their lives to some aspect of the arts. All these men (as well as other artists and musicians) became globally recognized, but who said that this is a requirement for a life purpose?

Jim Fixx authored *The Complete Book of Running* in 1977, documenting his running passion, and by popularizing the sport helped launch America's fitness revolution.

Ralph Nader became concerned with the safety record of American automobile manufacturers. After a journalistic expose of unsafe cars, Nader turned his passion for consumer protectionism into a lifetime purpose of advocacy for government reform.

John Harrison, a self-educated English carpenter, spent decades on a singular mission to develop a dependable chronometer, which is a type of marine clock so accurate that it can be used to calculate longitude while at sea. By successfully completing this task after many years of struggle, he revolutionized both timekeeping and sea travel.

Thomas Jefferson devoted his many talents to building the United States, and one of his main interests was gardening. Most people do not know that Jefferson was transfixed on the idea of introducing new crops and vegetables to America. Knowing that plants could transform society he saw his gardening of new varieties of fruits and vegetables as a patriotic mission. Jefferson therefore assembled a collection of vegetables at Monticello from virtually every western culture known at the time, and experimented with growing everything in order to find the most useful varieties for the American soil and climate. He ended up growing 330 different vegetables! When successful at growing a new species of edible he passed out the plant seeds and growing instructions to others with messianic fervor.

Jefferson wrote, "The greatest service which can be rendered any country is to add a useful plant to its culture." Jefferson pursued his efforts with vigor and saw them as the highest sort of patriotism. His work on determining which new plant species could be cultivated by farmers made a giant contribution to American farming and cuisine that most people don't even know about. For instance, we can say as a sort of summary that Jefferson helped introduce hot weather vegetables to southern eating.

Caesar Chavez, a Mexican American farm worker, saw first-hand the disadvantages and injustices suffered by Hispanic farm workers in America and out of these concerns co-founded the National Farm Workers Association (United Farm Workers). His life goal became making their struggle a moral cause and organizing them to achieve better working conditions. Practicing nonviolent forms of protest, such as fasting in imitation of Mahatma Gandhi, his efforts tremendously improved the conditions of farm workers and American agriculture.

George Washington Carver devoted himself to botany, and his teachings on crop rotation to improve soils lead to a higher quality of life for black farmers in the rural American South. Frustrated by the lack of hope displayed by many southern black farmers, Carver started a Farmers Institute to teach them better ways of farming. Although he only made $125 per month during his forty-seven years of work at the Tuskegee Institute, Carver turned down highly paid employment offers by Thomas Edison (for a $100,00 per year salary) and Henry Ford in order to continue teaching at Tuskegee, feeling that the need to help poor black farmers was more important than his salary. Carver made it his life's mission to improve the lives of southern black farmers and the economy of the South.

Ismael Ferreira, from the Brazilian state of Bahia, spent his childhood working as a sisal subsistence farmer in a region where most families were so poor that they lived in shacks without water or electricity. Lucky enough to go to college, upon graduating he determined that sisal farmers should no longer remain dirt poor, and made it his mission to put more money in farmer hands. He started organizing sisal farming cooperatives out of the 600,000 small producers in his state.

Ferreira spent four years working through bureaucratic labyrinths to finally succeed in winning his small producers an export permit giving them the right to export their sisal directly. Today the Small Farmers Association of the City of Valente (Associacao dos Pequenos Agricultores do Municipio de Valente) that he formed operates a factory that sells sisal ropes and rugs directly to U.S. and European retailers. It has brought more income to sisal growers and made a big impact in a region where hundreds of thousands of poor farmers earn part of their livelihood from sisal.

A life purpose does not have to produce results as large as those illustrated by these examples. These names were picked solely because some were recognizable, and they illustrate a wide variety of different interests people can have that may guide/occupy their lives, and sometimes even produce a large positive transformational influence. You don't need to have such grand aims. You simply must determine, though, what you want to do.

A life purpose does not have to deal with helping people or creating social change. With a life purpose you simply pursue *your own interests*. However, there are countless individuals in history who chose the calling to work for social change and who subsequently made a giant impact on the world.

For instance, Malala Yousafzai, although a simple Pakistanti schoolgirl, was shot in the head by the Taliban after she stood up for female education in her country. Upon recovering from surgery, she started devoting her life to becoming an activist for female education and women's rights. Her advocacy has won her a Nobel Prize and grown into an international movement for women's education and equal women's rights. Her inspiring story can be seen in the movie *He Named Me Malala*.

Susan B. Anthony was primarily a social reformer and women's rights activist who founded the suffrage movement in the United States, campaigning for women's right to vote. Despite constant obstructions and ridicule she pursued this mission until her death. Fourteen years afterwards the Nineteenth Amendment was finally passed, which was no doubt in part due to her ardent efforts.

Escaping slavery at the age of twenty, Frederick Douglass was probably the most influential African American of the nineteenth century. He devoted his life to the mission of ending slavery and gaining equal rights for African Americans.

B.R. Ambedkar "Babasaheb" was an Indian political reformer who spent his life campaigning for the rights of the untouchable caste of India. Vinoba Bhave was another Indian activist who started the Bhoodan land gift movement where landowners donated tracts of their personal land to India's landless poor including the untouchables.

Jane Addams, founder of Hull House and co-founder of the ACLU, is widely recognized as the founder of the social work profession in the United States. She saw it as her life's mission to devote her life to social reform, peace efforts, and the poor. For her efforts she became the first American woman to be awarded the Nobel Peace Prize.

These are just a few of the famous names who devoted their lives to social change. Once again, this does not have to be your life mission, although when you see social injustice then you should stand up in solidarity against it, as admirably taught in the Sikh religion. A life as a social reformer is a calling that requires caution because in many countries social reformers get thrown in jail, are persecuted or are killed. When I think about the perils of social reform, even to save the nation, the cautionary tale of the ancient Roman Gracchi family comes to mind.

The Gracchi family of ancient Rome had a mission of trying to transform Rome in order to save it. The brothers Tiberius and Gaius Gracchus both served as tribunes of Rome and devoted themselves to trying to reform Rome's problems involving the poor, the army, the holding of property, and the maintenance of the empire – all key issues for Rome's continued survival.

Tiberius Gracchus attempted to pass reform legislation that would redistribute the land holdings of aristocrats, the wealthy members of Rome's senatorial class, to war veterans and the urban poor who were languishing. Gaius Gracchus tried to pass a series of populist reforms that benefitted everyone, except the Senate because he gave greater power and riches to the equestrian class rather then Senatorial nobles. Both men were assassinated for their populist efforts at reform.

As a warning to all those who are good-hearted and wish to help mankind, the famous failures of the Gracchi has often been attributed to the fact they were too idealistic and overestimated the sacrifices others would be willing to make to cure Rome of its problems. In short, the two brothers lacked wisdom. Both were deaf and blind to the selfish aspects of human nature, especially in the Senatorial elite who opposed them, even though they tried to institute changes for the good of the country. Senators, seeing their own interests at risk, accordingly rose up and took the lives of these men when their own lands, money and power were threatened by reforms that were proposed for the benefit and survival of Rome itself.

Some individuals have taken it as their life's mission to pursue the safer avenue of advancing education instead of social reform. This educational mission can be seen in some of the following biographies.

The missionary Fred Laubach had a dream of ending illiteracy so he developed the "Each One Teach One" program used to teach over sixty million people to read in their own language. During his life he traveled all over the world speaking on the topics of literacy and world peace.

Thomas Gallaudet also devoted his life to education, but in this case to teaching the deaf. He founded the American School for the Deaf in Hartford, Connecticut, which was the first school for the deaf in America. His work was instrumental in the creation of American Sign Language. His lifetime efforts allowed the public to realize that the deaf could be educated, and it allowed them to be treated as equal members of the community.

Sequoyah performed an incredible act of merit by inventing and then spreading the Sequoyan syllabary for the Cherokee language. Through this syllabary he single-handedly brought literacy to the Cherokee nation and gave it the ability to not only communicate long distances but have Cherokee spoken words recorded for the ages. Of this accomplishment Sam Houston said, "Your invention of the alphabet is worth more to your people than two bags full of gold in the hands of every Cherokee."

Sarah Buell Hale is largely responsible for the Thanksgiving holiday becoming a national American celebration. She thought a national Thanksgiving would be a way to help unify all Americans, as well as a means for the country to joyfully acknowledge with gratitude the blessings of having a bountiful land. Therefore for seventeen years she advocated for the holiday, never ceasing in her efforts. She wrote letters to five Presidents of the United States - Presidents Taylor, Fillmore, Pierce, Buchanan and Lincoln – trying to persuade them to create a national Thanksgiving holiday, as a means of encouraging both gratitude and unity in the national American psyche. Upon receiving her letter, President Abraham Lincoln finally saw the wisdom of her suggestion because the holiday would help to unify America after the bloody Civil War, helping to "heal the wounds of the nation." Thus he proclaimed the last Thursday in November as an annual Thanksgiving holiday, which was due to her efforts.

While inspiring, many of these stories represent accomplishments far greater than many of us can make since we usually don't have such strong interests, commitments or ambitions. Furthermore, we aren't willing to make a career out of such interests anyway, and as a commitment they go way beyond our need to put bread on the table. That's okay. This is normal. Only certain people feel a passion for such commitments. Each of us has our own calling that we must find.

The point is not that these accomplishments are great or greater than most people are themselves willing to work for as a life's calling. The point is that they show sample paths of efforts that you yourself might contribute to helping, just as Sikhs are taught to do. Most people want to associate with something greater than themselves such as a worthy mission, and simply lending a hand or even donating a dollar or two to such people and efforts is something that can move us all forward.

Full of sound and fury, most lives lived signify nothing more than just consumption when there is a world of help that people can provide, even if it is but a single cup of water. What will others write on your tombstone if you didn't do anything to take care of others? Can you impact the greater community in any beneficial manner? Even if it is but a single step, can you not do something that will help improve the total lot of the world?

Until they identify a purpose or mission in life most people usually feel they are not complete. They feel like they are not doing what they were meant to be doing in the world. Hindus explain this as being due to the fact that they are "not following their dharma" or "not living in their dharma." If you are "following your dharma," however, then most people are very happy even if they do not have a lot of money. They are happy because they believe they are following their personal mission and life path, a purpose they have adopted or a reason for which they think they were born.

Some people choose their life purpose because of business pursuits or the desire for wealth. Some people make their family's care their life purpose. Some people devote themselves to a cause because they feel it is the right thing to do, such as there being a great need to fight some particular injustice. Some chose a life purpose out of feelings of compassion. Whatever the reason you should understand that a cause, mission, interest, vision or purpose in life gives it more meaning, so let me now introduce some individuals who found a life purpose in or because of their work.

Blake Mycoskie, founder of Toms Shoes, once visited Argentina where he encountered an American organization that provided shoes for children in need. He wrote in his book, *Start Something That Matters*, "It dramatically heightened my awareness. Yes, I knew somewhere in the back of my mind that poor children around the world often went barefoot, but now, for the first time, I saw the real effects of being shoeless: the blisters, the sores, the infections." He thereafter started donating shoes to those who could not afford them – one pair donated for every pair he sold, and since that time has given away over 60,000,000 pairs. Partnering with the Seva Foundation, he later started the "One for One" offering program for eyeglasses, providing eyeglasses or eyesight medical treatment for every pair of sunglasses he sold. This initiative has helped over 400,000 people.

The American actor Paul Newman enjoyed a very successful acting career, but founded Newman's Own on the whim of making salad dressing and donating all the profits to charity. This became a company whose two founding values were "100% of Profits to Charity" and "Quality Will Always Trump the Bottom Line."

Since its inception Newman's Own has branched out into making popcorn, spaghetti sauce, lemonade, and many other foods. Approximately 100% of the company's profits have turned into over $500 million in charity donations. Newman is particularly associated with opening up eleven Hole in the Wall camps that have helped hundreds of thousands of sick children with incurable diseases experience outdoor activities.

Scott Harrison, a former New York City nightclub promoter who one day had an epiphany that he "was selling selfishness and decadence," thereafter spent some time as a photojournalist for the Christian charity Mercy Ships in poverty stricken regions of Western Africa. He realized that most of the diseases they encountered were due to poor sanitation and the typical lack of availability of clean, safe water in developing nations. He thereafter vowed to devote his life to making a difference and thereafter founded the Charity: Water organization to help poor communities in developing nations gain access to clean water and sanitation services.

Confucius said that rich or poor, great or small, there is a Great Learning we must all pursue in life. He said that all people in life should devote themselves to a process of cultivating self-improvement that also includes practicing virtuous behavior and doing good deeds for others that improve their situation. Doing good deeds will produce an accumulation of merit for everyone so this mindset should become a natural part of everyone's life. From the habit of helping others as a basis, even though we might think we have but little to offer, the small acts of kindness from everyone in aggregate can transform the world into a better place. The great mass of what improves the world is due to just this – many tiny acts added together in unison.

By pursuing good deeds, self-perfection and self-improvement as a foundation, some individuals can have a larger than normal influence on their family, community, city, country, culture and even world. The primary unit upon which such positive influence depends is the single individual, *you*, who can cultivate yourself in certain directions and then band together with others of like mind (or simply support their efforts from afar) to create a stronger force for positive change. From one person you always move to a group whose aggregate influence is larger.

No one need wait a single moment to try to improve themselves or the world. We usually think that it takes tremendous efforts that are beyond us, but it only takes a little effort to work on ourselves, or support something larger than ourselves that we don't have to self-initiate. There are many ways to help some individual or a group achieve a better outcome for our community, city, country, state or world.

Robert Kennedy said, "Let no one be discouraged by the belief that there is nothing one person can do against the enormous array of the world's ills ... Each of us can work to change a small portion of events. And in the total of all those acts will be written the history of a generation." Margaret Mead said something even more compelling, "Never doubt that a small group of thoughtful, committed citizens can change the world; indeed, it's the only thing that ever has." Will you help others who are trying to make such efforts?

Positive change in the world starts with every individual who has a passion for a mission and then starts moving in that direction. One of the best things you can do for your children is to support the people and organizations that have such missions, and who are working to create a better world for your children and eventually *their* children. In fact, one of the most important things you can do for your family is to teach everyone they have an obligation to help others in less fortunate situations, and you can do this by supporting those working on the front lines and letting your own children see this. Besides teaching your children to create an outstanding life, to pursue a lifetime of learning, to care for the family and create desirable friendships, parents should also teach them to create merit for the family by helping others.

A family that adheres to strong values and these virtuous principles can influence its community to become better. A collection of communities can influence a country, and even a small group of countries can influence the world. As we will continually see, a great influence always starts with an individual or family who decides to do something about an issue.

Families and Larger Groups

Most people do not consider their purpose in life as their job or career.

Typically an occupation just makes money. The primarily focus or purpose for most of us usually falls squarely on taking care of ourselves and our family, and this *should* take top priority. Never forget this. Cover your home bases first and fulfill your familial obligations. However, even so occupied you can still make tiny but deft contributions for issues and causes that matter beyond the family and which accord with your higher aspirations. This is how to help move the world forward so that it doesn't stay too long at one stage of development.

Time, money and lack of interest prevent most people from spearheading world famous missions, and that's perfectly okay. We all have other concerns that are our top priority. We only cited these individuals as examples to spotlight the multitude of ways in which passions can become influences larger than anyone ever imagined. When a child sets up a lemonade stand in order to raise a little money for a charity, this is the type of heart that needs to be encouraged because this is exactly the spirit that will change the world.

Lack of free time and wealth (as well as interest) prohibit many people from following their dreams or passions or carving out a larger mission for their life, but in *Super Investing* I showed how an individual could accumulate enough wealth capital through tested investing techniques, which have worked over one hundred years, to create a legacy of prosperity that could last for several generations to fund philanthropic missions. In *Husbands and Wives Were Connected in the Past* I showed how to create strong families devoted to higher ideals regardless of one's religious affiliations. In *Color Me Confucius* I also recounted the teachings of Chinese Zen Master Yungu who taught Yuan Liao Fan how to change his personal fortune and destiny by improving his behavior through self-correction and by generating merit for the world.

Master Yungu had said, "Those who have millions of dollars in this life must have cultivated the good fortune worthy of that amount in the past. Those who have thousands of dollars must also have good fortune, which is worthy of generating that sum. Those, who die of starvation were in fact were meant to die in that manner. We must understand that their own past thoughts and actions created the fate of these people; the karmic result today is simply the fruit of their deeds. Heavenly beings do not have any intentions for us. ... If a person has accumulated enough merits and virtues for a hundred generations, then he or she will have descendants to last a hundred generations. One who accumulates enough merits and virtues to last ten generations will then have ten generations of descendants to live out that good fortune. The same goes for three generations or two generations. For those who have no descendants at all, it is because they have not accumulated enough good merits and virtues."

According to this traditional type of Chinese thinking, when a family dies out it is because its stock of merit earned from good deeds has run out. Its merit became depleted. Some families accumulate merit that will last for generations while others, just like countries, die off because of expending all their merit just as the third generation of a rich family, which did not build its fortune, also tends to squander its remaining store of wealth. According to eastern teachings, when a ruling dynasty falls, despite attempts to save itself, the fate of demise is also due to the fact that the merit of the dynasty has run out too. What usually brought a dynasty to collapse was an accumulation of improper actions, policies, excesses and errors due to a lack of wisdom, which is the product of deficient merit.

This is why not just individuals but families must work to always be replenishing their stock of merit rather than be using it up. Communities and states grow rich through adherence to prosperity principles, which is the road of merit accumulation as well. They accumulate merit slowly by adhering to virtuous principles of advance. Whether because of family traditions or religious teachings, family members must be taught that there are principles and values they should always uphold in their lives as well as things they should be willing to sacrifice for. Family members should be encouraged to practice ethical, virtuous behavior and participate in good deeds that help society. They should also try to build the family honor. One of the most important values within a family is the feeling of obligation to help others less fortunate who are in need, and a sense of civic duty and responsibility to improve the community situation. In Buddhism this is called "beautification" of the land you are in.

The ancient Athenian Oath encapsulated these principles. Those who recited it said, "We will never bring disgrace on this our City by an act of dishonesty or cowardice. We will fight for the ideals and Sacred Things of the City both alone and with many. We will revere and obey the City's laws, and will do our best to incite a like reverence and respect in those above us who are prone to annul them or set them at naught. We will strive unceasingly to quicken the public's sense of civic duty. Thus, in all these ways, we will transmit this City not only, not less, but greater and more beautiful than it was transmitted to us."

The next assemblage of like-minded people larger than a family is a group or community of some type united by common ideals and values. This includes friendly alliances such as "mastermind groups" of individuals united for a common interest. You can think of a mastermind group as an association of individuals with a common, similar purpose. When your personal aims are modest you can usually accomplish your goals by yourself but when they become elevated beyond a reasonable level you need to turn to a larger association of others, such as a mastermind group, church or your community to help achieve them. Thus we must talk about this higher level of assemblage than the family.

Mastermind groups are usually your first stop of greater community because they bring together people of like-minds and common interests. Napoleon Hill was the first to describe the great power of such mastermind groups, or associations of people united with a common intent such as Benjamin Franklin's Junto. The members of a mastermind group, or friendly alliance, come together in association in order to move forward on some common goal, purpose or objective. Napoleon Hill knew that some goals or objectives in life would fail if they were entirely dependent upon a single individual's sole efforts. Therefore he encouraged that harmonious groups of two or more people should be formed when individuals want to achieve a specific purpose or objective, and through this association the members should bring forth the power of camaraderie, mutual support and creativity to get something done that couldn't be achieved by one individual alone.

Confucius basically taught that after cultivating yourself you might become a role model of consummate behavior that could then influence such a group. Furthermore, larger and larger associations of like-minded people, banded together for common interests of improvement, could eventually influence a community, state, country and then the world. By uniting people under one umbrella this is how empires are formed.

People typically create mastermind groups to develop environments that solve problems or nurture and support growth in certain directions. To work well the group members should be friendly, growth-oriented and willing to share information among themselves. They should feel safe in their association with one another, cooperate with one another, and see a future to their efforts.

Each individual in the world has unique skills and resources they can contribute to such group efforts, and by banding together this is how a collection of individuals can achieve greater things. People united in a common cause, despite their differences, can be compared to a series of batteries connected to a single transmission line where each new individual can step up the total voltage and power. Each individual can stimulate all the others in unison.

From the power derived from associating with others, each of whom can contribute different ideas, energies, resources or efforts to a common cause, great things can be accomplished in the world. As Margaret Mead said, once again, "Never doubt that a small group of thoughtful, committed citizens can change the world; indeed, it's the only thing that ever has."

Even so, people get dismayed when there doesn't seem to be any progress in achieving what they desire even when they are ardently working towards its accomplishment. Perseverance, tenacity, patience, willpower and grit are the necessities that come to mind. They are characteristics we need to teach our children if we want them to succeed. The best advice I have ever seen along these lines comes from a response that coach Christopher Sommer wrote to Tim Ferriss when Ferriss impatiently queried when he would finally start seeing strength improvements from following the coach's exercise routine. The coach wrote back,

> Patience. Far too soon to expect strength improvements. Strength improvements (for a movement like this) take a minimum of 6 weeks. Any perceived improvements prior to that are simply the result of improved synaptic facilitation. In plain English, the central nervous system simply became more efficient at that particular movement with practice. This is, however, not to be confused with actual strength gains.
>
> Dealing with the temporary frustration of not making progress is an integral part of the path toward excellence. In fact, it is essential and something that every single elite athlete has had to learn to deal with. If the pursuit of excellence was easy, everyone would do it. In fact, this impatience in dealing with frustration is the primary reason that most people fail to achieve their goals. Unreasonable expectations timewise, resulting in unnecessary frustration, due to a perceived feeling of failure. Achieving the extraordinary is not a linear process.
>
> The secret is to show up, do the work, and go home.
>
> A blue collar work ethic married to indomitable will. It is literally that simple. Nothing interferes. Nothing can sway you from your purpose. Once the decision is made, simply refuse to budge. Refuge to compromise.
>
> And accept that quality long-term results require quality long-term focus. No emotion. No drama. No beating yourself up over small bumps in the road. Learn to enjoy and appreciate the process. This is especially important because you are going to spend far more time on the actual journey than with those all too brief moments of triumph at the end.
>
> Certainly celebrate the moments of triumph when they occur. More importantly, learn from defeats when they happen. In fact, if you are not encountering defeat on a fairly regular basis, you are not trying hard enough. And absolutely refuse to accept less than your best.
>
> Throw out a timeline. It will take what it takes.[24]

---

[24] Tim Ferriss, *Tools of Titans*, (Houghton Mifflin Harcourt, Boston, 2016), pp. 160-161.

Life Purpose

Many people want to do great things just on their own without being involved in a group, and that's fine too, but even lone wolves often need the support and encouragement of others. They might not ask for help so we must be the ones to identify the worthies who might need assistance but aren't asking, and then offer some help in a respectful way. This too is a type of merit-making. We already saw that Gandhi, who was nearly an ascetic, absolutely needed the support of rich industrialists to accomplish his mission.

Many people who set out to accomplish some mission are not very good at business or have no funds to support the valuable work they are doing, yet they still need outside assistance. The problem is that they might not ask for help, since this is often an embarrassing thing to do, so we might have to ask or volunteer for them.

One such needful individual was Luther Burbank, the "Wizard of Horticulture" who invented the blight-resistant Russet Burbank potato to help Ireland during the Irish potato famine. Since its invention it has become the most widely cultivated potato in the United States and the predominant potato for food processing in the world. Whenever you eat McDonald's french fries they are probably made from Russet Burbank potatoes. Burbank was so devoted to developing new crops to help mankind that he developed over 800 strains/varieties of plants over his 55-year career.

Unfortunately, Burbank had difficulties in supporting himself, which threatened the incredibly valuable work he was doing for America and world. He was never successful in his personal nursery business, but a donation by the Clarence McDowell Stark family and additional support by the Luther Burbank Society made his hybridization work to develop new plant species sustainable. In his revolutionary work Burbank eventually developed 120 different kinds of plums, 28 apples, 18 peaches, 500 hybrid roses, 30 cherries, 34 pears, and many other fruits and flowers for the benefit of mankind. This was all made possible due to the support of others who recognized his inability to finance himself.

Another individual who devoted himself to agriculture was Norman Bourlag, "the father of the green revolution." Bourlag won a Nobel Peace Prize for his contributions to feeding the world. He devoted his life to developing disease-resistant high-yield wheat varieties that vastly increased crop yields and improved food security in countless nations. Mexico, for instance, had been importing wheat and corn to feed its people but within a decade became a net grain exporter. For a time much of Bourlag's work was funded by the Ford and Rockefeller foundations that wisely decided to help the world by supporting his efforts. His work is credited with saving over a billion people from starvation, and he has been called "the man who has saved more lives than any other person who ever lived." The Ford and Rockefeller foundations helped make that possible.

Our great thanks and admiration should also be bestowed upon Sanjay Rajaram for developing 480 varieties of disease-resistant wheat that have been released in 51 countries to increase their wheat production, and Henry Beachell and Gurdev Khush for developing miracle rice varieties that have doubled the rice production in Asia since their development. Robert Chandler also led a team that developed tropical rice varieties that doubled and tripled the yield of traditional varieties of rice. The names of agricultural pioneers we must thank, who have silently helped save us from starvation, goes on and on.

Another individual devoted to a mission but who needed support was Dr. Paul Ehrlich, discover of the cure for syphilis, whose story was immortalized in the movie, *Dr. Ehrlich's Magic Bullet* starring Edgar G. Robinson. This movie recounted the passion of a man devoted to the new and revolutionary idea of developing chemical agents ("magic bullets") to internally fight infectious disease, and in particular the socially unmentionable disease of syphilis that was devastating societies.

While Ehrlich is the hero of the movie who finally found a syphilis remedy after 606 attempts, another unsung hero in the movie was Franziska Speyer, a Jewish banker's widow who was the one to fund his research to cure syphilis. In that era, an individual who donated money towards research on curing a socially unmentionable disease, where the research itself followed an unproven line of pursuit, would normally have been regarded as crazy, so she was the other real hero of the story. Her support required vision, commitment, courage and fearlessness too. She could not be the researcher or inventor herself, but without her support Ehrlich's great accomplishment would never have been achieved. Therefore she hugely shares in his great merit since she is the one who made it possible. The scourge of syphilis was not just cured by Dr. Paul Ehrlich but by Franziska Speyer!

The lesson is that if you cannot be the one to do the great deed(s) yourself then you can still earn great merit by supporting the direct doers in some way. Your support can range from the costless act of simply offering kind words to protecting the efforts, generating positive publicity, creating connections for it, or even providing some type of funding contribution although small. For instance, Mahatma Gandhi is greatly revered for helping lead India to independence. While he outwardly appeared simple and poor to the public he required lots of funding for his work. As one of the textile millionaires who help fund Gandhi and his entourage explained,

"It costs us a great deal of money to keep Gandhi in poverty." Gandhi's supporters earned tremendous merit by funding Gandhi, who was trailblazing the Indian movement for independence.

Another story of an unsung hero comes to mind, which is Commodore C.C. Wright Jr. who supported the weather engineering work of Trevor James Constable, allowing Constable to experiment with creating rainmaking equipment while at sea. Few know that Constable invented simple machines that could produce rain, a veritable godsend to humanity if his methods were ever studied and used on a larger scale. Tremendous merit goes to Constable for his relentless, single-minded pursuit of natural rainmaking secrets, but we should not also forget the man who supported his work of tinkering away while on ocean going vessels. Many people might have thought the Commodore a nut for giving permission and lending his support to Constable, just as Franziska Speyer might have earned criticism for supporting Dr. Ehrlich, but without this complementary support Constable would never have been able to produce his remarkable inventions.

Yet another great individual was Tirumalai Krishnamacharya, commonly considered the "father of modern yoga." He popularized yoga as a method of physical exercise, healing and spiritual practice. His students have helped yoga practice to spread across the world and include famous names such as B.K.S. Iyengar, A.G. Mohan, Srivatsa Ramaswami, K. Pattabhi Jois, T.K.V. Desikachar, and Indra Devi.

Despite great renown and celebrity for his accomplishments, when young Krishnamacharya was poor and penniless. Luckily he had the support of two great individuals in his life at important junctures. Once, in order to study with a famous yoga teacher (Yogeshwara Ramamohana Bramachari) he had to ask for travel permission from Lord Irwin, Viceroy of Simla, India. Being impressed with lad, the Viceroy not only made arrangements for Krishnamacharya to travel to Tibet to study with Bramachari but in generosity even supplied him with three aides and took care of the expenses.

The Maharaja of Mysore, Krishna Raja Wadiyar IV, also supported Krishnamacharya by having him teach yoga at the Mysore Palace. The Maharaja continually asked Krishnamacharya to go around India to give lectures and demonstrations on yoga, and asked him to open up a yoga school under his patronage. Without the Maharaja's support and patronage of Krishnamacharya's mission (which included publishing yoga texts and sending teams of teachers to surrounding areas), we would not have the popularity of yoga that we see today.

As you can see, a life purpose or mission can take on many different forms. As stated, this can be something as simple and mundane as taking care of your family, supporting your church and its efforts, or even building a business where you really want to make a difference. One could take on extra purposes such as coaching a local soccer team of young children in order to help them have fun and learn skills. It could be pursuing a hobby or other personal interest and using the skills and knowledge you develop to make a contribution to others in some way. When you develop useful skills you can always use them to contribute to an effort you deem worthwhile.

Become a Buddha, Bodhisattva or Guardian Spirit

There is a spiritual tradition across Asia that a man or woman who devotes himself or herself to a particular purpose or cause can become a Buddha or Bodhisattva guardian spirit/protector of that focus and others after their death. It is a matter of their interest and commitment. It is taught that people can use their greater spiritual capabilities in the afterlife to become a guardian protector of their country, city, community, religion and even institutions or causes. For instance, they can become a protector of a temple, family or even some special function or mission. Like a saint, they can train to learn skills and become a patron who can protect various entities or causes they deem worthy.

They can, for instance, become someone who helps human beings with healing by learning how to project their energy into sick people who are unwell. They can help educate children by giving them higher thoughts. They can help people to attain wealth by helping the right individuals connect with one another, giving them bright ideas or helping them make better decisions because of a knowledge of the future.

In *Buddha Yoga* I showed how one could even train to become a guardian spirit such as a:

Country (Nation-sustaining) protect god
City protect god (guardian spirit)
River or Ocean guardian spirit
Weather-ruling guardian spirit
Guardian spirit of a Religion
Temple or Sanctuary guardian spirit
Wisdom and Knowledge guardian spirit
Nature guardian spirit
Healing and Medicine guardian spirit
Military protector spirit
Justice guardian spirit
Wealth Generation guardian spirit
Travel Protection guardian spirit
Lake guardian spirit

Forest or Park guardian spirit
Agricultural guardian spirit
Music and Singing guardian spirit
...

Traditionally there are three requirements for becoming a Bodhisattva protector, guardian spirit, or "protector deity" after your death.

The first requirement, as taught in *Nyasa Yoga*, *The Little Book of Meditation* and *Color Me Confucius*, is that during life you need to cultivate meditation and inner energy work. You need to cultivate both your mind and body, your consciousness and your vital energy (Qi). You need to engage in a road of self-improvement that divinizes your mind and body, helping both to reach a higher stage of excellence. In particular, you need to cultivate virtuous behavior and values.

The second requirement is that you must show some degree of active interest in the type of guardian effort or patronage you are interested in developing. This could involve doing everything you can to familiarize yourself with some issue or mission, developing active skills in those directions, or contributing money to charities along those lines. In other words, you start to cultivate the qualities and skills of the Buddha, Bodhisattva or guardian spirit you want to become. For instance, if you want to become a guardian spirit involved with healing, like a Medicine Buddha, then you can charitably contribute to medical causes or start to learn various healing modalities yourself. We are all limited by circumstances such as a lack of time, money, energy or guidance, but you must make a vow of commitment and then start moving in that direction by taking whatever steps you can, however little, to start creating that future, even when you know that the final result is over the horizon. Every tiny step will count. That future *can* be created.

The third requirement is that you must make a personal vow that someday you will be big enough, powerful enough, or strong enough to be able to make a difference to lives in the area of your chosen interest, and ask Heaven to help you work towards this direction. You basically want to have enough *gravitas* (skills, resources, capital, standing, respect, support, etc.) so that you can accomplish whatever you want. Then you must start working to accumulate the tinder wood for that shining fire.

By devoting yourself even just a little bit to these three efforts right now, eastern traditions say you can start working towards becoming a guardian spirit, patron deity, protect god or protective deity after death. You can start developing skills in this life and continue developing those abilities after death to become a particular type of Buddha, Bodhisattva, Protect God or Guardian Spirit of your own choosing. It just depends on how and in what ways you want to make your life worthwhile, and what you want to do for the world. What type of light do you ultimately want to be?

10
WORLD PROSPERITY

"In ancient times, those who wished to make bright virtue brilliant in the world first ordered their states; those who wished to order their states first aligned (influenced) their families; those who wished to regulate their families first cultivated their persons; those who wished to cultivate themselves first rectified their minds; those who wished to rectify their minds first perfected the genuineness of their intentions; those who wished to perfect the genuineness of their intentions first extended their understanding; extending one's understanding lies in investigating things.

"Only after affairs have been investigated may one's understanding be fully extended to the utmost. Only after one's understanding is fully extended may one's intentions become perfectly genuine. Only after one's intentions are perfectly genuine may one's mind become rectified. Only after one's mind becomes rectified may one's person behavior become cultivated (refined). Only after one's person is cultivated may one's family be aligned. Only after one's family is aligned may one's state become ordered. Only after one's state becomes ordered may the world be set at peace."
- Confucius

As Confucius said, influencing others starts with an individual who learns about something or works on perfecting himself, and from there then proceeds to influence larger and larger groups of people - the family, community, state, country and even world. "To put the world in order, we must first put the nation in order; to put the nation in order, we must first put the family in order; to put the family in order; we must first cultivate our personal life; to first cultivate our personal life we must first set our minds correctly." In other words, changing the world starts with just one individual who perfects himself and then takes upon himself a mission by banding together with increasingly larger groups of men to bring about the effect desired.

A perfect example of the power and influence possible from just a small group of individuals is the Let's Do It! movement born in Estonia in 2008. Let's Do It! is a civic-led mass environmental cleanup effort that has engaged over 100 countries and 17 million people to date. It has become one of the fastest growing environmental movements in the world, and it all started with just a small group of committed men and women.

Here is the story. In 2007, a handful of Estonians became concerned that Estonia's forests were becoming polluted dumping grounds. They approached Rainer Nolvak, a tech entrepreneur, with an idea to solve Estonia's illegal waste and pollution problem in about five years with the help of volunteers. Nolvak clearly recognized the problem commenting, "I'm a solitary type of guy and I'm no longer alone in the woods – there was a remarkable amount of car tires, dressers and plastic bags. This combination felt violent. I thought that I should make one effort to change this – if it doesn't help, I guess I have to move to Mars."

With his help, the small group created a strategy and then brought in more volunteers to help plan their effort. They engaged over 500 official partners and organized a nationwide effort of communal work that motivated 50,000 people (4% of the Estonian population) to work together to clean Estonia in just five hours! This ended up removing 10,000 tons of garbage from Estonia's forests for less than 500,000 Euros. It is estimated that it would have taken the Estonian government three years and 22.5 million Euros to clean up the same amount of illegal garbage.

The news of this incredibly successful effort went viral. People from other countries started asking how they could also initiate a movement of voluntary collective action for cleaning up their own countries in one day too. Following Estonia's pattern, next Lithuania had a clean up day, then Latvia, Slovenia, Portugal, Serbia and other nations including even cities such as Bangalore and Delhi in India. The global request for assistance in developing these programs has resulted in a new effort christened as the Let's Do It! World program involving 150 countries.

Another example of the power of collective effort initiated by just a few people – in this case by *just one individual* - was the initiative spurred on by Verghese Kurien, the "Father of the White Revolution" in India. Kurien initiated "Operation Flood," the world's largest agricultural development program that eventually made dairy farming India's largest rural employer and largest self-sustaining industry. Relying on village dairy cooperatives he helped build from nothing, he transformed India from a milk-deficient nation that imported milk into the world's largest milk producer.

Kurien built an organization that changed India and brought prosperity to millions, including India as well. He organized millions of small farmers into successful cooperatives which followed the Anand management pattern that let poor farmers handle their own affairs. In other words, rather than having the government or businessmen run the cooperatives, farmers in each region became the owners of their own cooperative, thus cutting out the normal middlemen. Kurien often said that replicating the Anand pattern across the country was his life mission.

Using this pattern of cooperatives, where Indians of different castes and classes learned to forget differences and work together due to the motivations of economics, he also made India self-sufficient in edible oils too. Kurien's emphasis on the production of products by the masses, instead of accepting the mass produced imports from other nations, has lifted millions out of poverty in India. He is now recognized as one of the greatest proponents in the world of the power of grass roots cooperatives.

Accion International, a non-profit charity, has made it possible for all of us to participate in similar forms of impact investing because it often funds the creation of cooperatives, which it helps guide to fruition, and other programs that bring people out of poverty.

Dr. Govindaoppa Venkataswamy, inspired by the sage Sri Aurobindo, had a different vision that started just with himself. His dream, which became his life purpose and mission, was to make low-cost to no-cost eye care available to the Indian masses (who live on less than $2 per day). He took on a mission "to eradicate needless blindness" so he set the goal to give sight back to the 12 million people in India suffering from cataracts and preventable blindness. People might scoff at such audacity, but where there is a will there is a way, and he has made incredible strides in accomplishing this.

After retiring at age 58, and despite rheumatoid arthritis misshaping his hands, with this goal in his heart he founded what has become the Aravind Eye Hospitals that have had a gigantic impact in eradicating cataract blindness in India and the world. Run mostly by Venkataswamy's siblings and their spouses, they are now one of the biggest networks of eye hospitals in the world and perform nearly 50% of eye surgeries within India.

Dr. Venkataswamy's mission was to have Aravind perform cataract surgeries on a large scale with the treatments being free to the poor while being subsidized by paying patients. Therefore he developed a new health care model whose efficiencies allowed paying patients to subsidize the free ones, but they still paid less than they would at other Indian hospitals.

Since this would only be possible if his eye hospitals were extremely efficient, Venkataswamy searched for efficiency lessons everywhere and even attended McDonald's Hamburger University to learn about the company's assembly line efficiencies, standardization practices, strict quality control, and ruthless cost control. Venkataswamy would even follow catering people around in five star hotels or walk around with janitors at airports to see how they would clean toilets, each time looking for principles of productivity and efficiency that he could apply to his hospital. It is said that Aravind can practice compassion only because it is run like an efficient McDonald's assembly line with a sustainable business model. The high volume of operations is the key to its being able to offer free health care. This is because the fixed building and staff costs are the same no matter how many surgeries are performed, so to reduce the cost per patient it needs to help as many patients as possible.

Because of his age and eccentric philanthropic business model, banks refused to lend money to build the very first Aravind eye hospital. "You are too old," they said, or "You want to operate for free on patients who cannot pay. This isn't a business model we can fund." Dr. Venkataswamy and his siblings therefore mortgaged their houses and pawned their jewels to pay for the construction of the first Aravind hospital that had just eleven beds. When the construction was done they moved in furniture from their own homes.

Starting from a humble first hospital, Aravind has now treated more than 30 million patients and has performed more than 4 million surgeries. It now has five hospitals in different locations with over 4,000 beds. Aravind even produces its own intra-ocular lenses and other ophthalmic supplies in order to save costs, and makes them available to other organizations. About 300 eye hospitals in India and in other countries are now using the Aravind model, which started because of the vision of a single individual who wanted to serve India.

While Aravind extends an invitation for all to come and be healed of blindness, it originally found that only 7% of villagers who needed eye care were coming to get help. Therefore, to help the countryside villages it established storefront vision centers in rural areas and communities. It also established "moving camps" that visit villages every few months to offer eye exams, basic treatments and free glasses. By concentrating on rural villages with a successful eye care system, Aravind has ended up helping all of India and influencing other nations with its successful model.

Another project, which has spurred the microfinance and microcredit boom across the world that has the potential to help countless millions break out of poverty, is the Grameen ("Village") Bank created by Professor Muhammad Yunus in Bangladesh. Yunus and the Grameem Bank he founded were awarded the Nobel Prize in 2006 "for their efforts through microcredit to create economic and social development from below."

During visits to the poorest households in the Bangladesh village of Jobra near Chittagong University, Yunus found that village women who were making bamboo furniture had to take predatory high-interest rate loans to buy their bamboo and then repay most of their profits to the money lenders. Trapped in this high cost debt circuit, they could never get ahead. Traditional banks did not want to make tiny loans at reasonable interest to such entrepreneurs due to the administration costs and high risks of default, so Yunus lent US$27 of his own money to 42 women in the village to break them out of this debt cycle. Thus he initiated the worldwide practice of microcredit.

Since those initial loans, Grameen Bank was eventually developed to continue this mission and has secured microloans for over nine million borrowers with a repayment rate of 99.6%. It has become active in 97% of Bangladesh villages, thus greatly affecting the country, and has been imitated across the world. Access to credit for poor entrepreneurs in villages is based upon the very reasonable terms of group-lending and weekly-installment payments.

To ensure repayment of its microloans, groups of individuals (a "solidarity") apply together for the loans and its members act as co-guarantors of repayment. Group members encourage each other to repay, and also support one another in their entrepreneurial path of development. Without this "solidarity lending," which imposes more discipline upon borrowers than "bond of association" lending, many individuals would not have borrowed at all or would have been forced to continue relying on loan sharks for their credit needs.

Yunus remarked on the dynamics of lending to groups, "... Group membership not only creates support and protection but also smooths out the erratic behavior patterns of individual members, making each borrower more reliable in the process. Subtle and at times not-so-subtle peer pressure keeps each group member in line with the broader objectives of the credit program. ... Because the group approves the loan request of each member, the group assumes moral responsibility for the loan. If any member of the group gets into trouble, the group usually comes forward to help."[25]

The Grameen Bank was founded upon the principle that loans are better than charity for helping people escape poverty, which is a self-help principle that the early American philanthropists also learned through many painful failures. Grameen has made loans available to various underserved classes of society – women, the poor, the illiterate and unemployed – and those loans have helped them achieve dramatically better lives.

---

[25] Muhammad Yunus (with Alan Jolis), *Banker to the Poor: Micro-lending and the Battle Against World Poverty*, (Public Affairs, New York, 1999), pp. 62-63.

What's interesting about Grameen Bank is its emphasis on spreading the principles of prosperity among its clientele, which we can say is a focus on eliminating the causes of poverty. Upon taking a loan, every borrower recites the Sixteen Decisions of the Grameen Bank and vows to follow them, which are as follows:

We shall follow and advance the four principles of Grameen Bank: Discipline, Unity, Courage and Hard work – in all walks of our lives.

Prosperity we shall bring to our families.

We shall not live in dilapidated houses. We shall repair our houses and work towards constructing new houses at the earliest.

We shall grow vegetables all the year round. We shall eat plenty of them and sell the surplus.

During the planting seasons, we shall plant as many seedlings as possible.

We shall plan to keep our families small. We shall minimise our expenditures. We shall look after our health.

We shall educate our children and ensure that they can earn to pay for their education.

We shall always keep our children and the environment clean.

We shall build and use pit-latrines.

We shall drink water from tubewells. If it is not available, we shall boil water or use alum.

We shall not take any dowry at our sons' weddings, neither shall we give any dowry at our daughters' weddings. We shall keep our centre free from the curse of dowry. We shall not practice child marriage.

We shall not inflict any injustice on anyone, neither shall we allow anyone to do so.

We shall collectively undertake bigger investments for higher incomes.

We shall always be ready to help each other. If anyone is in difficulty, we shall all help him or her.

If we come to know of any breach of discipline in any centre, we shall all go there and help restore discipline.

We shall take part in all social activities collectively.

By emphasizing this prosperity code the Grameen Bank has tried to promulgate a mindset and encourage specific activities that will eliminate the causes of poverty. For instance, by stressing hygiene the result has been a reduction in disease and early deaths. By stressing that children go to school the result has been that nearly every loan recipient has school-age children enrolled in regular classes. The fact that even girls receive an education is one of the well-known principles for reducing global poverty.

Grameen Bank says that over half of its borrowers in Bangladesh have risen out of poverty due to their loan as measured by the following standards: all school age children of the household attend school, all members of the household eat three emails per day, the borrower's household has clean drinking water and a sanitary toilet available, the house is rainproof, and they have the ability to repay a US$4 loan.

Conforming to the values of the Sixteen Decisions is a discipline that builds the merit/habits that will break people out of poverty. Yunus has said that the poor are like a miniature "bonsai tree" and can accomplish great things if they just get access to the credit that can help them become self-sufficient and improve their own conditions. Due to its success, over time the bank has branched off into supplying other services to the poor such as supporting village phone programs, housing loans, and related anti-poverty ventures.

Since its inception, the success of the microfinance model has spread everywhere and inspired similar efforts in dozens of countries. It has even inspired the creation of non-profit organizations, such as Kiva Microloans (Kiva.org) which allows ordinary individuals to themselves lend money via the internet to low-income entrepreneurs in over 80 countries using Paypal. Kiva also started with humble beginnings – seven loans totaling $3,500 that were all repaid within six month's time.

Since its founding in 2005 by Matt Flannery and Jessica Jackley, Kiva has crowd-funded more than a million microloans totaling over $1 billion, mostly going to women. The lives of countless families, and especially women since they receive the majority of loans, have been transformed through the many microfinance institutions that Kiva sponsors. These microfinance partners have provided loans enabling families to establish or better finance businesses, grow more agricultural crops, educate their children, renovate their homes, and buy medicines or medical services.

I love the Kiva system so much that I have used it to provide over 1,000 microloans myself to individuals all over the world and encourage you to check it out. I encourage you to check it out. Kiva is another example of how a simple idea by a couple can spread across communities and throughout countries to have a net impact that transforms the world.

Another effort to help villages originated with Sajay Bunker Roy, who wanted to come up with alternative ways to address India's poverty and inequality issues, especially the need to empower women. Roy decided to make it his mission in life to help solve these problems. For his solution he created the Barefoot College, which teaches uneducated and semi-literate people in village communities a variety of careers that help sustain the local economy and community. The major principle of the college is to train individuals, especially women, to help Indian villages become self-reliant. To help India, Bunker Roy is operating at the village community level.

Barefoot College participates in various projects such as rainwater harvesting (instead of digging wells that soon run dry), solar energy installations, and education such as teaching midwifery, doctoring and more to community residents. Much of the teaching (including lessons in reading, writing and accounting) takes place via night schools because students are too busy during the day.

One of the most well-known projects is "solar engineering" where women who can neither read nor write are taught how to install and maintain solar panels that keep rural villages supplied with electricity. By teaching women these jobs that were normally performed by men, it created a sense of empowerment because their involvement greatly benefitted their community. The website of the BarefootCollege.org explains,

> To "demystify and decentralize" solar power, we are building capacity at the village level by training rural, illiterate and semi-literate women to build, install, maintain, and repair solar electrification systems in off-grid villages. Participants from developing countries of Africa, America, Asia and the Pacific Islands are trained for six months at the Barefoot College campus in Tilonia, Rajasthan. The women build solar electrification systems (e.g. LED Lamp, Charge Controller, Home Lighting System, Solar Lantern) during the program. The equipment they build is shipped to their villages where it is used to electrify the houses in their community. They also learn how to set up a 'Rural Electronic Workshop' (REW) in their villages to store components and equipment needed for the repair and maintenance of the solar units. The Barefoot College approach involves only practice and no theory and thus the trainees need no educational qualifications. Additionally, Barefoot solar engineers learn by seeing and doing, without the use of language, other than learning the English names of essential parts (e.g. capacitor, resistor).

Since its establishment, the Barefoot College has expanded to more than 70 countries and trains villages in countries such as Ethiopia, Senegal, Bhutan, and Sierra Leone.

Switching continents, across sub-Saharan Africa it is the small farmer who is the bedrock of the regional and national economies. One of his greatest risks is drought; if the rain does not fall then his crops will fail. In a bad season with no rainfall, farmers can lose their entire harvest and will then be in debt, lacking the money to buy seeds and fertilizer for the next growing season.

The non-profit Syngenta Foundation for Sustainable Agriculture, a spinoff from the global agribusiness giant Syngenta AG, was founded with the objective to "work with rural communities in the Semi-Arid regions of the world and improve their livelihoods." It helped sponsor an ingenious solution, namely crop microinsurance, to help deal with this issue.

As Rose Goslinga explained in a popular TED talk ("Crop Insurance, An Idea Worth Seeding"), the Syngenta Foundation sponsors smallholder crop insurance that has insured hundreds of thousands of farmers in Kenya and Rwanda (and now India) against drought. Currently dozens of projects are being led by the World Bank to develop this type of insurance.

Here is how it works, and note the brilliant use of technology to solve problems which otherwise would be too costly to manage. Bags of seeds are priced with the cost of insurance baked in and insurance cards are inserted into those seed bags. Farmers opening the bags register for the insurance by calling a toll-free number and giving the unique code on the inserted insurance card, receiving immediate policy confirmation by phone text message. Using GPS coordinates, the call also registers the farm's location and allocates it to a weather satellite pixel.

Crop insurance is normally managed through farm visits and inspections by insurance professionals, but this would be uneconomical in many rural communities. Therefore the insurance companies turned to the technology of satellite imagery for a solution. If satellite images showed that too little rain fell during the subsequent weeks after planting when crops were supposed to germinate, farmers with insurance are *automatically* sent new bags of seed (or repayment). No one need file for any claim as everything is done automatically.

As practiced in India for seed corn, when there is no rain the insurance company initiates the claim process by immediately transferring money to the farmer's bank account for the seed corn purchased so that they can buy new seed and plant again. This simple mechanism that links together an insurance company, insurance broker, weather data, call center and seed company has provided a lifeline to vulnerable farmers.

Yet another organization formed to end hunger and poverty around the world uses the interesting route of providing free livestock and training to struggling communities. This charitable organization is Heifer International. Heifer is the outgrowth of the efforts of one man who was lacking in finance and logistics, but persevered to get started with his vision.

Heifer began in the mind of an Ohio famer named Dan West who was directing a program in Spain supplying hungry children with milk during the Spanish Civil War. Thinking about his own daughters being healthy and well-fed back in the States, West believed he should start some type of process that would bring that same wellness to Spain. West observed that as fast as you give milk to the children they drink it and it is gone, and it is economically prohibitive to import milk to a war-torn nation engaged in the costs of recovery. West started thinking, "These children don't need a cup of milk, they need a cow," and upon his return to the U.S. took this idea to his church and neighbors. West asked his church community and neighboring farmers to donate pregnant dairy cows so that poor families could have milk for years. Together they donated the first seventeen heifers to Puerto Rico, and West's ideas became the nucleus of Heifer International.

Since its inception in 1944, Heifer has provided oxen, water buffalos, pigs, goats, llamas, alpacas, sheep, chickens, rabbits, ducks, bees, and fish to over 20 million families (over 100 million people) in more than 125 countries worldwide. Today Heifer does much more than just distribute livestock. It has gone beyond helping individual families because it has adopted a community-focused process that helps communities build markets and food security.

Part of the Heifer charitable model for building the prosperity of families and communities is the brilliant idea that the recipient of an animal must also pass on the gift they receive. For instance, a milk cow is given to a family under the condition that its offspring must also be given to another family who would, in turn, give a calf to yet another family and so on. In this way, the gift is passed on forever and donors to Heifer are actually sponsoring a gift that keeps on giving, which is why I love making gifts to Heifer myself.

While Grameen Bank has its sixteen principles of prosperity, Heifer International has Twelve Cornerstones of Just and Sustainable Development, which form the acronym "P.A.S.S.I.N.G. G.I.F.T.S.," that it uses as a framework to ground all of its decisions about projects. In other words, all gifting projects are aligned with the principles of P-Passing on the Gift, A-Accountability, S-Sharing and Caring, S-Sustainability and Self-Reliance, I-Improved Animal Management, N-Nutrition and Income, G-Gender and Family Focus, G-Genuine Need and Justice, I-Improving the Environment, F-Full Participation, T-Training, E-Education and Communication, and S-Spirituality. A fuller explanation of these principles is as follows:

Passing on the gift allows families and individuals who have received animals to be donors themselves.

Accountability allows for organization at the grassroots level. Community members decide together what kind of animal and assistance they would like. They also set goals, plan appropriate strategies to achieve those goals, and evaluate their success. Participants take responsibility for making the most of the tools and training they receive.

Sharing and caring. Participants become donors themselves and contribute to a more unified community.

Sustainability and self-reliance. Heifer training empowers participants to take charge of their own success; each project has an exit strategy to prepare farmers for self-sufficiency.

Improved animal management. Project participants learn all essential aspects of animal husbandry.

Nutrition and income are the rewards Heifer expects recipients to gain from their gift animal through the consumption and/or sale of animal products.

Gender and family focus encourages women and men to share in decision-making and community development.

Genuine need and justice. Ensures that those most in need are given priority in receiving animals and training.

Improving the environment includes such agroecological techniques as improving soil fertility with animal manure, promoting forestation, respecting and encouraging biodiversity, monitoring watershed conditions and minimizing erosion.

Full participation is expected within the groups that Heifer works with.

Training and education include formal sessions as well as informal farm visits and demonstrations. Each project group decides on its own training needs and local people are involved as trainers.

Spirituality is expressed in common values, common beliefs about the value and meaning of all life, a sense of connectedness to the earth, and a shared vision of the future.[26]

The point of these stories is that individuals, families or even churches are small groups of people but they took upon themselves a mission that involved helping individuals, villages or communities to end the causes of poverty and suffering and establish the foundations of prosperity for the poor. Sometimes those efforts were so successful at generating prosperity that they were duplicated across the world.

These stories not only illustrate how a single man's vision and efforts can change a country, but *how people can band together in communities* to strengthen and upgrade their joint fortunes (which is the basis of labor unions, cartels, and trade associations), and how improvements experienced

---

[26] "Heifer International," *Wikipedia: The Free Encyclopedia,* Accessed July 17, 2018, from en.wikipedia.org/wiki/Heifer_International.

by countless communities in aggregate can change the fate of a nation. When an idea is especially useful it can pass beyond the borders of a country and transform the world.

As Confucius stated, from the individual an influences passes to the family, village, community, state and then world. Individual people work on improving themselves, create change and bring new embellishments to culture and civilization. This is also called beautification or betterment.

What bands people together is a cooperative spirit of trying to help one another to uplift circumstances, even when difficult, which is the definition of generating merit. You lift the fortunes of all through the practices of philanthropy, charity, sacrifice, discipline, cooperation and giving whether that giving is of teachings; material goods, money or resources; or confidence and fearlessness. When this type of helpful, cooperative spirit declines then culture and prosperity decline because it directly affects the strength of society's asabiya. However, when a group of people together align themselves with greater principles of virtue, such as the principles of prosperity promoted by the Grameen Bank, the principles of aid promoted by Heifer International, or others, the net result can be a stronger community and greater whole.

In *War and Peace and War*, Peter Turchin explained his belief that the fall of the Roman empire was also paralleled by a decline in Roman virtues, which the Romans called *mos maiorum*. Turchin explains,

"The early Romans developed a set of values, called *mos maiorum* (ancestral custom), which governed their private and public lives. Probably the most important value was *virtus* (virtue), which derived from the word *vir* (man) and embodied all the qualities of a true man as a member of society. *Virtus* included the ability to distinguish between good and evil and to act in ways that promoted good, and especially the common good. It also meant the devotion to one's family and community, and heroism in war. Unlike the Greeks, the Romans did not stress individual prowess and excellence, as exhibited by Homeric heroes or Olympic champions. The Roman ideal of the hero was one whose courage, wisdom, and self-sacrifice saved his country in a time of peril. 'Who with the prospect of death, envy, and punishment staring him in the face, does not hesitate to defend the Republic, he truly can be reckoned a *vir*,' says Cicero. Young men were taught that it was 'sweet and glorious to die for one's country.'

"Other important Roman virtues included piety, faith, gravity, and constancy. Piety (*pieas*) was a family virtue – devotion and loyalty by men and women to the family group, willing acceptance of parental authority. It also meant reverence to the gods, expressed through performance of required religious rites and ceremonies, such as the sacrifice of a ram to Janus, or a heifer to Jupiter. Even the infamous gladiatorial fights evolved from an ancient religious ritual involving sacrifice of prisoners to the dead.

"Faith (*fides*) meant keeping one's word, paying one's debts, and fulfilling obligations toward people and gods. Violation of *fides* was an offense against both community and gods. Gravity (*gravitas*) meant discipline, absolute self-control – a dignified, serious, and calm attitude toward both good and bad fortune. Constancy (*Constantia*) was a related virtue of perseverance, doing what was necessary and right, even under the most trying circumstances. Romans greatly prided themselves on moderation, the avoidance of all kinds of extremes and excesses, and remarked on any instances of immoderate behavior in themselves and in other peoples with disapproval. …

"Roman values were part of *religiones* – literally, bonds that held the community together. The ancients recognized the importance of religion in strengthening the state. Socrates reportedly said, 'Those who honor the gods most finely with choruses are best in war.' Polybius, personally skeptical of religious metaphysics, thought that it played an important role in keeping the masses under control. In general, Roman religion extolled the virtues of hard work, discipline, duty, loyalty, and courage. Religion was the glue that cemented the people together and gave the early Roman society an extremely high degree of asabiya. The cohesiveness of the society was so high that until the first century B.C. Romans did not need a police force to keep public order. The internally motivated discipline of early Romans, the formalized and ritualized behaviors of their culture, was enough to maintain public order. …

"One cannot overemphasize the importance of these personal qualities of early Romans to their subsequent rise as an imperial nation. Note how the Roman virtues served to limit individualism (gravity and constancy), strengthened ties within family (piety) and community (faith), and sacrifice for the common good (*virtus*). Romans had no physical or technological advantage over the peoples they conquered. An average Roman was smaller and weaker than an average Gaul. In a one-to-one duel, an average Roman would most likely lose to an average Gaul. On the other hand, a hundred Romans could hold even against a hundred of Gauls, and ten thousand Romans would easily defeat a Gallic army many times their number.

"But even this comparison is somewhat misleading, because curiously enough, the Romans were pretty lousy at winning battles. The typical sequence of any war between the Romans and their numerous opponents was to lose battles early in the war, but then, nevertheless, win the war. As Livy said, 'That lot has been given to us by some fate that in all great wars, having been defeated, we prevail.' If the first war was lost, the Romans tried again and again, until they won. (This is a reflection of the Roman virtue of constancy, of course.)"[27]

Livy, who wrote an account of Rome's early founders because he wanted to call Romans back to the virtues of their ancestors, also firmly believed that Rome's decline was due to an erosion of the morality of its populace. He wrote in the preface to his *History of Rome* that one could see a gradual decline in Roman morals matching the decline in the Republic: "Let the reader observe what life and morals were like (then) and through what men and by what policies in peace and war the empire was established and enlarged. Then let him note how discipline gradually declined so that our morals began to degenerate, slowly at first and then more and more rapidly, until as we reach the present times they plummet precipitously until we can neither endure our vices nor their cures."[28]

Turchin goes on to say that the vertical integration of Roman society, which involved a strong degree of solidarity felt between the commons and the elite aristocracy, was one of the most important explanations for Rome's success at empire building. If there had been glaring barriers between the classes then class conflicts would have broken out and caused revolutions by the commons.

There are two special factors to note, which many neglect, when we want to explain the rise of the Romans who built an empire and conquered the world. The first was the internal cohesiveness of the Romans, and second was the remarkable openness of the Romans to incorporate other peoples into their fold as Chinese culture did in order to survive, evolve and thrive. Both factors, argues Turchin, are necessary for being able to build a world empire.

And so we have come full circle from the fate of cultures and civilizations to empires and countries, to cities, to companies and their products, to men and their decisions to be good or bad, and then once again to greater communities or groups of men who band together out of virtuous longing to work in associations that change the world for the better. Even companies thrive due to adopting a meritorious guiding vision of providing some sort of service to customers, while products succeed as long as they embody the virtue of satisfying customer needs and desires. Individuals can choose to act virtuously in the world or without morals, and the positive path is to associate with larger and larger groups of like-minded ethical people in order to create greatness.

Back we come to the building of culture and civilization again, and the

---

[27] Peter Turchin, *War and Peace and War: The Rise and Fall of Empires*, (Plume, New York, 2007), pp. 155-158.

[28] Gregory S. Aldrete, "Why the Roman Republic Collapsed," Class lecture, The Rise of Rome, TheGreatCourses.com.

message that it all depends upon a strong foundation of virtue or *virtus*. It all depends upon a group effort to move things forward for the better, but a movement starts with solitary individuals who are inspired to make a difference.

Countries are built by culture, civilization is built by culture, culture is built by the virtues we emphasize. For instance, the Kingdom of Prussia once became an undisputed military might in Europe by consistently emphasizing "Prussian virtues," born of Lutheranism and Calvinism and the German character, that were slanted towards a military ethos. The typical Prussian virtues, which revolve around the Christian concept of good works and the Protestant idea that work is a duty that benefits the individual and society as a whole, include austerity or thrift, courage, determination, discipline, fortitude without self-pity, frankness, Godliness, humility or modesty, incorruptibility, industriousness or diligence, loyalty, obedience, punctuality, reliability, restraint, self-denial, self-effacement, sense of duty, sense of justice, sense of order, sincerity, straightness or straightforwardness, subordination and toughness. Contrast this military ethos flavored with a self-responsibility theme with pacifistic Buddhism. As a religion, Buddhism developed its own characteristic flavoring that perfumes its adherents due to an emphasis on the Paramitas (perfections) of generosity or giving, discipline (proper conduct that refrains from harm), patience/endurance, vigor/energy and diligence, meditation and wisdom. If you continually emphasize certain selected values or virtues, you will shape a country, culture, civilization or empire in a certain way that will determine its trajectory and ultimate fate. For instance, if you soak a piece of meat in sauce overnight, it will absorb the flavor of that seasoning according to the length of absorption and strength of the flavor. By emphasizing virtues and values, you will create a bias in a group of men over time.

As Benjamin Franklin showed, you absolutely *can* cultivate virtue personally for yourself such as the *virtus* within the *mos maiorum*. The community can help you cultivate certain traits and you can work to cultivate them yourself. As Archibald Leach said about crafting his skills to become the actor Cary Grant, "To a certain extent I did eventually become the character I was playing. I played at being someone I wanted to be until I became that person, or he became me." Like Cary Grant, you can cultivate yourself to become anything you want, and cultivate to become however you wish to be.

You certainly can cultivate virtues by working at it. Benjamin Franklin explained how to do this in his *On The Art of Virtue*, whose methods and those of others I painstakingly detailed in *Color Me Confucius*. Writing as a preface, Franklin explained that the problem in cultivating virtue is that few know the means to do so, which is why he recorded his own methodology for posterity:

Many people lead bad lives that would gladly lead good ones, but do not know *how* to make the change. They frequently *resolved* and *endeavoured* it; but in vain, because their endeavors have not been properly conducted. To expect people to be good, to be just, to be temperate, &c., without *showing* them *how* they should *become* so, seems like the ineffectual charity mentioned by the Apostle, which consists in saying to the hungry, the cold, and the naked, "Be ye fed, be ye warmed, be ye clothed," without showing them how they should get food, fire, or clothing.

Most people have naturally *some* virtues, but none have naturally *all* the virtues. To *acquire* those that are wanting, and secure what we acquire, as well as those we have naturally, is as properly an art as painting navigation, or architecture. If a man would become a painter, navigator, or architect, it is not enough that he is *advised* to be one, that he is *convinced* by the arguments of his advisor that it would be for his advantage to be one, but he must also be taught the principles of the art, be shown all the methods of working, and how to acquire the habits of using properly all the instruments; and thus regularly and gradually he arrives, by practice, at some perfection in the art. If he does not proceed thus, he is apt to meet with difficulties that discourage him, and make him drop the pursuit.

In one sense much of the progress we have surveyed can be viewed as a product of decisions about character, values and virtuous behavior. This includes the importance of positive character traits for getting ahead and producing better states for the world such as hard work, perseverance, sacrifice, concentration, discipline and charity. In another sense it can be viewed as about making wise decisions that produce merit, such as aligning with the trends, cycles or principles of prosperity. In yet another sense it can be viewed as all about behavior, whether profit-seeking or altruistic, that works to create a benefit for a greater collection of individuals all the way up to the world.

The question then is, "Going forward what will you do now? What direction will you choose when you have decisions to make? How has this discussion helped you?"

Much of the good or bad in the world happens as a result of decisions men make to pursue either consummate conduct or selfish self-interest. Which direction will you choose? What standards will you apply to your own decisions and behavior going forward?

Now is the time to consider what you want as the components of your own *mos maiorum*, your own set of behavioral principles and values you want to cultivate and instill in your life. Have you included any space in our life for the cultivation of virtue and merit? Are your current passions worthy of you, and does what you want to accomplish in life reflect the highest and best you along with the highest and purest of aspirations? Do you have to rearrange your life to give space to any light you want to bring to the world?

In city branding and product branding you want to represent items in a beneficial way that highlights their virtues *because they are that way*. Similarly, we all make reputations for ourselves. However, you can change your reputation by cultivating your personality, ordinary behavior and efforts in the world. You can and should choose what you personally want to become, and be known for, and work to excel at that so that you become that. How you behave and what you work on is how you will become known. You must figure out yourself what should be included within your own vision of a noble better self, your own *mos maiorum*, and from this as a foundation take firmer steps to establish your personality and life in the way you want.

Plutarch, in his *Lives of the Noble Greeks and Romans,* provides case study biographies which illustrate how men can excel in greatness or error. The premise of Plutarch is that tales of the excellent can lift the ambitions of men and women who study them, and inspire similar greatness.

Livy also once wrote, "The study of history is especially healthy and profitable for the following reason. In history, you see examples of every sort of behavior displayed before you, and from these you can identify for yourself and your country good things to imitate and shameful things to avoid." Therefore, the focus now is on yourself and what you will do moving forwards. The task before you is to determine what you should personally cultivate in your life.

In all of this I ask you to remember a single but most important guiding principle. The survival as well as the ultimate greatness of cultures, civilizations, empires, countries, cities, companies, people, families, communities, and missions are linked by a common theme. The common standard within the successes is an adherence to uplifting virtues, ethics, values, merit or morality that supplies the causes of ascension and longevity. For happiness, success, prosperity or whatever is deemed the greatest and most auspicious, you have to align yourself with this principle of behavior.

ABOUT THE AUTHOR

Bill Bodri is an ex-Wall Streeter who holds Masters degrees in engineering, business and clinical nutrition. He is the author of a number of books including:

- *Super Investing: 5 Proven Methods for Beating the Market and Retiring Rich*
- *Breakthrough Strategies of Wall Street Traders*
- *Bankism: How the Government's Bank-First Policies are Destroying the Nation and How to Survive the Aftermath of a Coming Dollar Collapse*
- *The American Reader*
- *Sport Visualization for the Elite Athlete*
- *Visualization Power*
- *Detox Cleanse Your Body Quickly and Completely*
- *Look Younger, Live Longer: Reverse the Aging Process in One Year Using Eastern Traditions and Modern Nutritional Science*
- *Super Cancer Fighters*
- *Color Me Confucius*
- *Quick, Fast, Done: Simple Time Management Secrets from Some of History's Greatest Leaders*
- *Move Forward: Powerful Strategies for Creating Better Outcomes in Life*
- *Buddha Yoga*

www.ingramcontent.com/pod-product-compliance
Lightning Source LLC
Chambersburg PA
CBHW070726220326

41598CB00024BA/3319